Gracie & Albert

Cheryl Grant Gillespie

ANDROSCOGGIN PRESS

Androscoggin Press, West Kennebunk, ME

© 2019 Cheryl Grant Gillespie

Gillespie, Cheryl, 1952-
Gracie & Albert / Cheryl Grant Gillespie

All rights reserved. No part of this book may be reproduced, displayed, modified, or distributed by any means (electronic, mechanical, photocopying, recording, or otherwise) without the express prior written permission of the copyright holder, with the exception of brief quotations included in reviews.

Publisher's Note: This is a work of creative non-fiction. Facts have been slightly embellished to develop a narrative sense. Some names of supporting characters have been changed.

For further information and permission approval or to order copies of this book, go to https://cheryl-writes.com.

First edition, Androscoggin Press Printing, 2019

ISBN # 978-7329471-2-2

Printed in the United States of America

Dedication

To Mom and Dad

Chapter One

Shit! Shit! Shit! Flashes of bright light blinded Gracie when she dared to open her eyes. She peeked again. Stained ceiling flashed above her. *Jesus H. Christ! Where the hell am I?* Gracie tried to rub her eyes. She couldn't. Her arms wouldn't move. She glanced down at her right side. Leather straps? Some kind of stiff jacket? People bumped into whatever she was rolling on. How many? Two? Three? Uniforms? White uniforms? Garbled talking. Gracie struggled to decipher what they were saying. Were they talking to her? Strong smells. Bleach, urine, sweat. *Better hide inside,* Gracie told herself.

How did I get here? She tugged again at her arms and then looked down. Her arms were across her chest and tethered down. She started fighting the restraints as much as she could.

"Mrs. Grant, Mrs. Grant, please be calm. You're safe now," a strange voice said.

Gracie kept pulling at the restraints.

"My dear, now please settle down."

Gracie didn't know this person talking.

"Mrs. Grant, Grace, you're safe. You're here in the hospital. Shush now."

Gracie started rocking her head frantically and moaned as she did so.

"Please, Grace. I'll get a doctor," said the strange voice and then silence.

Gracie lay still and searched her recent memory. A scene played out in her head. She was standing in front of the open attic window. She knew those people were watching her. She could feel it. They'd been after her for a while now. She took in the nighttime quiet of the big boarding house at Boutelle Avenue where she and Albert were staying. *I've had enough. Can't do this anymore,* she thought. With her husband snoring in the bed behind her, she pushed out the screen of the window until it was loose on the bottom. She squirmed herself through the window, under the flapping screen, and out onto the roof. *Enough.* Gracie scooted herself down to the edge of the roof. She heard Albert whisper, "Gracie?"

Do it now! She pushed herself off. Blissful falling. Then one bump and blackness. Albert screamed from the high window. Quiet, then Mrs. Alley hovered over her face. Blackness again. Hazy memory of riding and riding in a big vehicle. People talking. Struggling to get people away. Fighting as hard as she could with everyone even though her head hurt. Albert crying near her then being pulled away. Being jostled around and then a jab in her behind. Blackness. *What had gone wrong?*

The person who had spoken earlier reappeared with a tall man. *A doctor?* Gracie made out the female voice saying to him, "This is Grace Grant, twenty-three, attempted suicide victim. Uncooperative in the ambulance and upon arrival, so she was restrained and drugged. She came to just a few minutes ago and is still agitated."

Attempted? Shit!

The tall man's face was close to her face now. "Mrs. Grant, Grace?"

Gracie peeked back at the man and then closed her eyes, pulled at the restraints, and grimaced. *Go away. Leave me alone. Leave me be.*

"Grace? Gracie?"

Gracie stopped writhing against whatever was tethering her and looked up at the man's face.

"Gracie," said the man, "you're safe and in a hospital. The nurse and I are here to help you. Do you understand me? Gracie, can you understand what I'm saying to you? We're here to help you. Gracie?"

For a few seconds, Gracie stared at the man. *Shit! A doctor and a nurse. Oh, good God!* Then she resumed her struggle.

Gracie heard bits of a discussion about phenobarbital and needles and the patient hurting herself. Then she felt a pinch and blackness enveloped her.

Chapter Two

Albert looked up at the Augusta State Hospital. Tears blurred his vision. The stone building, outlined by vast green lawns, stood on a hill overlooking downtown Augusta, Maine and the Kennebec River that curved through it. Albert thought this deceptively elegant stone edifice looked like a hall at an Ivy League college that he had only seen pictures of in magazines. Then he shivered as he remembered going in the less-than-grand back entrance earlier to follow the stretcher with his wife strapped to it. He knew the bleak insides of the hospital in no way matched the front façade.

"Come on, Al, I've got to get back to the kids. Work won't do itself, you know," said Mrs. Alley, grabbing Al's right forearm with a sturdy squeeze. "Drive me home, please."

Albert wiped his damp face with the cuff of his shirt and got into his baker's truck. He'd take Mrs. Alley back to her house on Boutelle Avenue, pick up his bread and donut deliveries from the bakery' and do his route. Mrs. Alley was a tiny, female mighty-mo. Albert had no idea how old she was. She rode shotgun silently this day, gripping the side door handle of the truck. The seats were so high they prevented her feet from touching the floor, even with the very tips of her toes. Albert was the only young person to call Mrs. Alley just Alley to her face. She had a soft spot for Albert. Even his wife Gracie didn't dare call her that.

Consumed with the image of his Gracie's face twisted in fear, Albert missed a yield sign on the rotary leaving Augusta, and horns blared at him.

"Jesus, Al, I know you must be upset, kid, but killing us ain't gonna do no one any good!" said Mrs. Alley.

"She didn't say anything, Alley, not a thing." Albert gripped the steering wheel at ten o'clock and two o'clock. "How could she go from my sweet Gracie to the person we just left in that hospital in a matter of a few weeks? I just don't get it."

"Al, that's why we brought her there. We didn't know what to do with her. Did you want her to try to do herself in again? I don't know about you, but two attempts was enough for me. Lord only knows how she managed to get that screen loose and jump off the roof as weak as she was last night!"

Albert's grip tightened on the steering wheel. "God, Alley, I know, but I hate myself right now for leaving her there. And what will I do with the boys? You can't watch them forever."

"Worry about work this morning, Al, and then go down to see your sister and mother this evening. Family helps family. Stay the night in Portland if you need to."

"You've done enough for us already. I'll pick the boys up after work and take them with me. My mother will take care of them."

Mrs. Alley said nothing. She smiled at young Albert.

Albert appreciated the extent of what Mrs. Alley had done for them. He had run to her with Gracie and their two young boys when he didn't know what else to do. Mrs. Alley took them all in and even cared for Gracie, Wayne, and Stevie while Albert tried to hang onto his job. The past couple of weeks with Gracie had been like caring for a ninety-pound, uncontrollable baby. She wouldn't eat, wouldn't talk. Wet and messed herself, and fought anyone who tried to clean her up. Albert glanced at Mrs. Alley and thought she looked relieved. It was too much.

The fifteen mile drive from Augusta to Waterville seemed to take forever. Albert was lost in worry about how his life had fallen apart. He knew Mrs. Alley probably worried about work left undone in her home laundry business. The foster children she took in made messes while she was consumed with trying to care for Gracie and their two baby boys as well. He felt pangs of guilt.

Chapter Three

Gracie opened her eyes and looked around. *I'll keep quiet this time, damn it all.* She could feel her arms were still tied down. She could wiggle her toes but barely move her legs. There were other straps she couldn't see. The room she was in was cavernous, with unappealing green walls pocked by random stains and dings. A light hanging down from the blotchy ceiling glared in her eyes, so she turned her head to one side. It was then she saw the curious windows. Thick, wire screens were *inside* the windows blocking any chance of a decent view outside. The screens were held in place by huge screws. She'd never seen screws so big. Gracie tried to remember where someone had told her she was. *Is this a hospital? Is that what those screens are all about?*

God, there were no security window screens that could help her, she fussed to herself. It got in her head and couldn't be stopped. She needed thick screens installed in her head. Chaos seeped out of her through her mouth, her eyes, and everywhere it could. It scared her. It controlled her.

The sand dunes she had erected around herself to try to escape this horror also kept her from the world. Too many flare-ups for her to crawl over the dunes. She hid behind them. This presence was a challenging roommate. She tried to appease it by vacating her small shell, but she kept being brought back, damn it all. Couldn't the creatures on the other side of the dunes see she'd had enough? They wouldn't leave. Wouldn't leave her alone. Life without them would be a breeze. A breeze she hadn't felt in a long time.

She was tired of trying to control it. Trying to keep people from noticing it. When she let it rage, trouble pursued her. *Better lie still. Be still, so it thinks it's in control.* Plan her next attempt to escape better than the times before, so this time she would be free. It's been too much. Too much to live with. Too much to handle.

"Oooooooh," sighed Gracie.

"Gracie, you're awake. Good morning!" said a voice that sounded somewhat familiar. "I'm Nurse Downer. Remember me? Are you hungry? I could see if it's all right to untie your restraints so that you could eat. Let me check with one of the head nurses. Be sure and tell whoever comes back with me that you'll be a good girl now."

Good girl, thought Gracie. *Where am I? Why would someone be speaking to me this way?* Gracie promised herself again that she would be quiet.

"Mrs. Grant, glad you are back in the land of the living, my dear," announced an older nurse who appeared at her bedside. "Can we trust that you'll cooperate with us now? Can we take these restraints off without any trouble? Grace, can you hear me?"

Gracie just glared up at the nurse with her teeth clenched so tightly it hurt her jaw.

"Good heavens, how old is this little thing. She looks no more than a child. Where's her chart?" said the older nurse. "Grace Grant, you're not doing yourself any favors by not speaking. Grace, can you hear me? Does she talk?"

"Dr. Knowles couldn't get her to respond earlier this morning."

"I'll see if I can find an intern or some orders," said the older nurse as she left.

"Grace, Grace, you really need to talk," said Nurse Downer to Gracie.

Gracie scowled up at her and then turned her head away. She was stirred a few minutes later by a new person appearing.

"Hello, Miss Deaner Downer, sweet Duner Downer," cooed a tall man, as he wrapped his arm around the young nurse who was standing at the side of Gracie's bed. "What do we have here?"

"Oh, Dr. Getchell, thank goodness you're here. What should we do? Mrs. Wight doesn't know if we should take her restraints off, but how will she eat?"

"Refusing to talk now, are you? My, you could be a pretty one if you weren't all mussed up! Lord, what do you suppose this scar is from?" said Dr. Getchell as he reached out and stroked the left side of Gracie's face. Gracie flinched and hissed at the doctor. "Okay, she can hear us, now can't you, sweet thing. What did you say her name was? Lord, I suppose I could read that chart. Miss Dooner, would you be so kind as to read the chart to me, please?"

Gracie listened to the young nurse read to this doctor. "Poor, dear thing!" sighed Miss Downer upon finishing the last sentence. "What will we do with her?"

"We'll start by getting this straight jacket off her. She's probably scared to death. Sidle up next to me for protection in case this little, wild thing decides to lash out, Miss Donner."

"Dooctoor Getchell, you know my name is Downer, now cut it out!"

Gracie moved submissively as the doctor pulled the jacket off her. She immediately tried to cover herself as she was clad only in a faded, thin nightgown. The doctor and nurse watched as she did this. She stared back at them.

"Doctor, remember where the notes said that she responded to 'Gracie'?" cooed the nurse in Dr. Getchell's ear.

"I'd respond to anything that you blow in my ear like that," chimed the doctor.

"I'm talking about the patient!"

"Gracie, Gracie, Gracie..." sang Dr. Getchell watching for a reaction. "She's giving us the silent treatment, I'm afraid. Bring her something to eat. Let's give her time. We'll find out what her story is soon, I'm sure."

"Is it okay to leave her unrestrained, doctor?"

"We'll find out, now won't we, Miss Dunner Dooner. Call an attendant if you need one to help with her. Gotta run!"

Within a few minutes, Miss Downer had placed a tray table with a lunch consisting of soup, toast, and milk at Gracie's side. "Let's just sit you up, so you can eat, now," said the nurse, giving her a slightly concerned look. "Now, Gracie, you really need to start eating and responding. Come, now, eat!"

Gracie turned her face away. *I wish this thing would just leave me alone,* thought Gracie. *Please just let me float along in my own misery.*

"Gracie, I have other patients. Now let's start eating."

Gracie gave no response. She wouldn't even look at the nurse now.

"Okay, your bed straps are going on. I've got to get to some others now."

Gracie lay quietly in the bed with her arms and legs strapped down. *What in God's name am I going to do now? What will they eventually do to me? I don't care. I just don't care. Life is not worth living anymore.*

Gracie lay like this, refusing to eat or communicate for the next forty-eight hours. Miss Downer became angry with her the fourth or fifth time she wet herself and her bedding required changing. "The least you could do is point to the bathroom. I know you can hear me!" she scolded.

"What are you scolding her about?" asked Dr. Getchell, strolling in as Miss Downer was finishing the most recent bedding change. "Is there anything new here?"

"Dr. Getchell, she won't even tell us when she needs to use the bathroom. She hasn't eaten anything solid. She'll let me give her a bit of milk. That's all. What are we looking at here anyway?"

"Not to worry. Let me confer with the mighty Dr. Knowles before a final decision is made, but I think a course or two of electroshock therapy is what is indicated here. Let me have a minute with her alone, please."

After Miss Downer exited the room, Dr. Getchell hovered over Gracie's face. He let his right hand stroke her chin a couple of times. Gracie stirred slightly but then immediately stared back at him with a blank expression. The doctor then caressed Gracie's neck and upper chest. Slowly, he moved his hand down over her right breast. Gracie gritted her teeth. Otherwise she didn't react.

"Not much in that department," remarked the doctor as he pulled his hand away. The patient and doctor stared at one another for an uncomfortable moment, and then Dr. Getchell strutted out of the room.

Chapter Four

"Mother, what will I do if you don't take the boys for me? Please?" Albert stood inside his sister's front door in Portland with one sleepy tow-headed toddler at his feet and a bald baby snuggled on his shoulder. He pressed his face against his sleeping Stevie's head to try to cover up the tears in his own eyes.

"Just come on in, Al, it's late. We'll talk this out. Have you even had any supper?" asked Ava Grant as she grabbed Stevie out of his father's arms.

"Didn't have time. Went right from work to pick up the boys and drove on down here."

Ava stooped down to peek at little Wayne. "You hungry?" she asked.

"Yes," replied the little guy to his grandmother.

"Mother, what's going on down here? I'm trying to get to sleep," said Mollie entering the front room in pajamas and housecoat. Albert's sister glanced around and produced a suspicious look. "Oh, dear, what has happened now, Albert?"

"I'm getting these three boys something to eat, Mollie. You go back to bed if you need to for work tomorrow. I'll handle this," replied Ava.

"Right, and you'll do this in my apartment, I suppose," said Mollie.

Albert said nothing. He watched his mother take his boys into the kitchen and looked back at his sister. He was too tired to argue with her.

"Where's Gracie?" asked Mollie.

"Can we talk about this in the morning, Sis? I'm hungry."

"Oh, this doesn't sound good. You look like death warmed over, Al. Let's go in the kitchen. Maybe some warm milk will give me a chance of getting back to sleep. Guess I don't need to hear details tonight. It's a good thing you are my darling baby brother, and I love you."

Dr. Knowles took a deep breath and exhaled slowly before he answered the call on his office line the next morning. "Hello, how may I help you?"

"Well, doctor, you have my Gracie in there. I need to know if you can help her, sir," replied Albert.

"And what is your name?"

"Albert Grant. You have my wife Gracie in your hospital. A nurse told me you could maybe tell me something about her."

"When did she come in?"

"Two days ago. Early in the morning."

"Oh, yes, I remember her."

"How's she doing?"

"We just received her. It will take a while to diagnose Mrs. Grant."

"Do you think you can help her, sir? Do you?"

"Now, now, it is 1948. Things in the psychiatric field have much advanced, Mr. Grant. I'm confident we will be able to make headway with your young wife."

"Yes, sir, but how long will this take? We have two sons still in diapers. It's hard to cope with them and work. I really need Gracie to get well."

"Do you have some help?"

"I do, but I don't know for how long. How long does this type of thing take, sir?"

"Listen, son, you hang on, and we'll do our best to help your wife."

"Your nurse says I can't visit her."

"We don't recommend visits right away. It would interfere with the treatment. We'll let you know when you can come visit."

There was silence on the line. "Mr. Grant, Al, are you there? Have I answered all your questions?"

"I'm so sorry I had to leave my Gracie there, sir."

"You did the right thing, son. Now take care of yourself and your boys, and I'll call you again as soon as possible with an update. Can you do that?"

"Yes, sir, I guess I can. Thank you."

Chapter Five

As hard as she struggled to focus, Gracie could not grasp how long she had been in this nasty place or why. People and things floated around her like a nightmare. She tried not to talk and give herself away, but she had to move around.

"Al, Al, did you put the boys to bed?" Gracie whispered out the large, institutional window. "Where are you?"

"Did you hear her? She can talk. I knew it!" said Miss Downer to her supervising nurse as they glanced over at Gracie.

"I didn't hear a thing. Won't talk when I speak to her, that's for damned sure," replied the senior nurse struggling with a medicine cart behind Miss Downer. "Spends her time standing in the middle of the ward floor looking petrified as she wets herself or gazes out that window."

"I heard her, Mrs. Wight. Be right back."

Gracie jumped when Miss Downer touched her forearm. "Gracie, who is out the window?"

Gracie stared blankly at her.

"I heard you talking just now, Gracie."

"I don't want to die now," whispered Gracie.

"What? Of course you don't. Knew you could talk."

"Don't let them take my boys," said Gracie a little louder.

"Why would anyone do that, Gracie?" replied Miss Downer.

"I need to go home. Need to take care of my boys. Where's Al?" Suddenly, Gracie shrank away from Miss Downer as she glanced over the nurse's shoulder. Mrs. Wight looked at Gracie with a knowing nod. Gracie hustled to her bed and laid down with her face to the wall.

That evening, Gracie refused to eat supper. Miss Downer started to feed her as she had been doing until Mrs. Wight observed them and said, "Let's let this one decide she is going to eat, Nurse Downer. You have several patients in need of your help."

"But, Mrs. Wight, she's thin enough. It won't take me but a minute. She only eats a few bites."

"Leave her alone tonight, Miss Downer. Let's see what she does."

An orderly took away Gracie's untouched tray two hours later.

Gracie was at the window of the ward the next morning when Nurse Wight found her. "Grace, we need to take you down to x-ray today," announced the no-nonsense nurse. "Let's go now." When she grabbed Gracie's left arm, Gracie knelt to the floor in front of her.

"Please don't take my boys! Please!" said Gracie.

"Child, no one is going to take your boys. I'm taking you down to have an x-ray," Mrs. Wight said, pulling Gracie's arm to help her up.

Gracie broke from the nurse and ran across the ward. Dodging beds and patients less nimble than her current quarry, the nurse went after her. A male attendant came into the ward upon hearing the noises some of the unsettled patients were making as they watched the encounter between Gracie and Nurse Wight.

"Mrs. Wight, let me grab her for you," said the attendant. He managed to hold her for a couple seconds, but she broke free and continued to run around. A game-like atmosphere took over the ward as some patients cheered Gracie on while others rocked back and forth in agitation.

"Holler for help!" said the attendant while he tried desperately for a second time to hold Gracie. "Damn, she bit me!" Applause was heard then as Mrs. Wight called for another attendant.

Two attendants and the nurse managed to lead Gracie out of the ward and down the hall to the x-ray room. She was returned to her bed later in a sedated state. She missed supper again.

Chapter Six

It was too hot at Mrs. Alley's laundry that late summer day. Three girls had messed up shirts on the mangle because of fussing about the heat while trying to press, so Mrs. Alley herself had taken over the hot monster. She fumed to herself about paying these young things good money to just sort and fold clothes. Little Gracie, all one hundred pounds of her, had been able to handle that mangle. She was also good with the state children. Gracie came to stay with Mrs. Alley and her husband Charles when she was just eighteen. She worked in the laundry and the house, and wasn't shy about hard work. She had done plenty of it in the past six years at her uncle's farm, Gracie had informed her. When she told Mrs. Alley that her mother died when she was only sixteen, the older lady softened to her like she hadn't with most of her other hired girls. Gracie was a joy to have in the house, and Mrs. Alley missed her when she married Albert even though she grew to like the young fellow. Now this misfortune had fallen on these sweet folks. Mrs. Alley didn't understand how God could let something like this happen to such a dear, hardworking couple of kids.

Lost in thought about Gracie being in the hospital that sweltering afternoon, Mrs. Alley almost singed two white shirts herself. The ringing of the phone caused her to jerk the mangle cover up and save them. No one answered the phone. Of course, Mrs. Alley almost snatched bald any employee who did pick it up and say hello, so she was left scurrying for it herself.

"Alley's Laundry."

"Hello? Hello?"

"Alley's Laundry, God damn it! Who's calling?"

"This is Dr. Kenneth Knowles from Augusta State Hospital looking for Albert Grant," said the doctor.

"Oh, please, sir, please forgive my French. Just so busy today. Al is staying here, but he's at work. Can I take a message?" replied Mrs. Alley.

"Yes, please have him call us at the hospital at his earliest convenience."

"Is Gracie okay, sir?"

"To whom am I speaking, please?" quizzed the doctor.

"Doctor, I was taking care of Gracie before we finally gave up and brought her down to you. I'm so worried about her, sir. How is she doing?"

"Are you the Mrs. Alley who gave testimony at the patient's intake?"

"Yes, sir. Gracie's like a daughter to me."

"Well, then I guess no harm will be done in letting you know that she is doing a bit better. I really do need to speak to her husband to give an official diagnosis. If he could call me as soon as possible, please."

"Doctor, I'll be sure to tell him to call. Poor thing has been worried to death about her."

"Thank you, ma'am. Goodbye."

"Bye, Doctor," said Mrs. Alley, hanging up the phone. She sat down and let herself rest just a little before returning to badgering the girls about working faster on the laundry mangle.

Albert complained to Mrs. Alley about the hospital being a long distance call. With her encouragement, he finally gave in and dialed the number the doctor had left.

"Mr. Grant, how long has your wife not been herself?" asked Dr. Knowles once greetings had been taken care of.

"Please, sir, you can call me Al. Well, she's been poorly for a while now, Doctor."

"How long has it been since she talked sensibly, Al?"

"You see, it didn't happen all at once. She got worse in degrees, so it's hard to pinpoint, Doc."

"Let's put it this way. When did you notice something was wrong with your wife?"

"She started talking crazy stuff 'bout four months ago, sir. Talked about people being after her and stuff for a while before she actually stopped talking much. Other people started noticing and talking to me about it. I didn't know what to do with her."

"How long has it been since she stopped taking care of her personal hygiene?"

"Maybe two months now."

"You've had a hard time of it, Al."

"I just need her to be better, Doc. Can you help her?"

"It may take a while. I need to have you come down to the hospital and sign for some specific treatments. Is that possible soon?"

"Sure, but Doc, I can't afford anything fancy. I might have to pay to have my boys cared for while I work. I'm pretty tapped out as it is."

"We'll see what we can do for you, Al. We'll treat Gracie."

"How long do you think this might take?"

"She's been sick for a while. It will take a while to get her better, Al. Come down as soon as possible to sign some papers, please."

"I'll get down tomorrow after work, sir."

"Take care, son."

Mrs. Alley stood with her hand on Albert's shoulder as he still hung on to the phone he had just hung up. "I'm so sorry, Al."

"Alley, my mother and sister can't handle the boys much longer. The doctor says Gracie could be in there for a while."

"Go get them and bring'em here. Keeps this mess of foster kids busy to play with them, anyway."

"I'll try to pay you something."

"We'll worry about that later. Go get Wayne and Stevie, and you plan on staying here full-time yourself for a while longer, too. We got room, and the boys will want their dad."

Albert put his head in his hands and cried.

Chapter Seven

"I need to go home," said Gracie to the young nurse as she placed a tray in front of her.

"Gracie, what have I told you? You need to start responding to the doctors when they try to talk to you. You also need to start eating on your own. Three meals a day and not just bites and glasses of milk," replied Miss Downer.

"I'll be good now. I feel fine. My boys need me. Please!"

"Good, Gracie. Then eat!" The nurse walked away, leaving her with her tray.

Gracie sat on her bed with her tray untouched and looked around at the people in this large ward she was in. *What kind of a hellhole is this place? I'll sit still and not cause any trouble. I'll just float.*

"Mrs. Grant, you need to eat," said Mrs. Wight, startling Gracie into banging against her tray as she hadn't seen the senior nurse approaching. "Ninety-five pounds is not enough weight on your frame. Your blood pressure is sky high and your coloring is horrible. Don't you want to get better, child?"

"I need to get out of this dishpan alley!" said Gracie to the nurse. "Where's my coat and hat, please?"

"Child, they're in the check-in office, but you won't be needing them soon at the rate you're going."

Without thinking, Gracie knocked the meal tray off her stand. She sat rigidly on her bed and glared at Mrs. Wight.

"Attendant!" hollered Mrs. Wight. "Need help here."

Gracie was grabbed by a male attendant who looked to Mrs. Wight for directions. Gracie squirmed in his grip.

"Take Mrs. Grant to Section III and please sedate her if necessary. We've had enough of her uncooperative behavior today, thank you."

Gracie awoke later to the chatter of Miss Downer.

"Gracie, what am I going to do with you? You're not ever going to win a battle against Nurse Wight. That old lady is set in her ways, you know. Handsome Dr. Getchell always says, 'That old bat must have come over on the Mayflower!' He's so funny. I know you're awake. Saw your eyes look up at me. Now here is what we're going to do. I'm going to get an attendant to sneak you back to the ward. Wight has finished her shift for the day. You are going to start behaving, you hear me?"

Gracie did not respond positively. She didn't refuse either. She watched as Miss Downer charmed an attendant into helping her roll the gurney Grace was strapped to back to the ward she had been in before.

"Gracie, do we have an understanding? I'm letting you out of your restraints now. You'll get me in trouble if you don't behave. "

"Why do I have to sacrifice? I don't want to die," whispered Gracie.

"Don't be silly, Gracie. You are fine now. Settle in on your bed for me."

Gracie managed a weak smile back at Miss Downer. It worked. She disappeared from Gracie's sight, and Gracie was free in the ward again. She sat on her bed for a long time watching the other patients. She knelt beside her bed and tried to pray. *God, why have you trapped me in this forsaken hole?* It was then she felt someone actually watching her. She glanced up and noticed a young, blond woman. The woman smiled at her. Gracie thought of going over to her bed which was a couple beds from her own.

As Gracie started to get up, she heard Miss Downer's ever cheerful voice say, "Cheryl Lee, time for your session with the doctor. You don't want to keep Dr. Getchell waiting. Come along."

The young nurse had Cheryl Lee by the left elbow and was swiftly leading her out, but the patient managed to glance back at Gracie with a distraught look. Gracie settled on her bed and got lost in her thoughts again. When her supper tray was delivered, Gracie tried to eat some of the food. It was dreadful, but she felt a bit better all the same. *Silly little Nurse Downer will be thrilled with me!* Then she waited.

A couple hours after trays had been collected, patients on the ward seemed to settle. One attendant sat in a distant corner and read a magazine, Gracie noticed. She studied the area by the door. Then she got up and stole quietly to it. She slipped out of it without the attendant even looking up from his reading. Scooting down the hall, she looked for an office that might contain patients' belongings. She was peeking in her third room when she heard the chatter.

"Dr. Getchell, you know I'm not that type of girl!" remarked a very familiar voice.

"Now, now, Miss Dooner Deener, what are you thinking? I was only having a little fun with you. Come on back here!"

Then Miss Downer was in the hall looking at Gracie. "Lord above, what will we do with you, Gracie?"

"Problem?" asked Dr. Getchell as he appeared in the doorway of the room Miss Downer had just come out from. "Did you forget to lock the ward door again?"

"Don't fuss, Dr. Getchell, I can handle Gracie. She responds well to me. I'll get her back to the ward. Gracie, Gracie, Gracie," the nurse chanted as she led a compliant patient back to her ward. "You don't want to do this, Gracie. You won't like what they might do to you."

Chapter Eight

"Say, Al…" began Phil as the work day at Harris Bakery was coming to an end for both of them. He strolled over to Albert as he was arranging his racks in the back of his bakery truck. "What's up with Gracie? Heard she's in the hospital. Know she's been poorly for a while now."

"Oh, yep, she's down in Augusta, Phil," replied Albert.

"Heavens, why down there? Couldn't they do something for her right here in Waterville?"

"Well, it's complicated. She needs a special treatment they don't do up here."

"Which hospital is she in, Al?"

"She's at Augusta State for a specific reason."

"God, Al, someone in the office said that this morning, but I didn't believe it. Our sweet little Gracie? Why there?"

"Phil, I don't think it is everyone's business, but if you must know, the family doctor thinks she has a blood clot on the base of her brain. Causing her to act funny and black out a bit. It's serious."

"Oh, well I knew it had to be something like that. She didn't just go off the deep end. Not the Gracie I know; so sweet and bright. But there's been talk, Al."

"About what, for God's sake?"

"'Bout her acting funny and all."

"Well, damn it. Set people straight when you hear them talking from now on. My Gracie's not crazier than anyone else. Doctor says she'll be fine as soon as she gets this treatment. And it's no business of anyone's in that damned bakery."

"Sure, I'm sorry. You know what we've always said. World's full of assholes, and it's our job to keep them supplied with bread and donuts." Phil patted Albert on the back and said his goodbye. Albert watched him drive away in his truck.

Later that evening, Albert sat in a kitchen rocking chair. With a sleeping Stevie in his arms, he started talking to Mrs. Alley, who was finishing up supper dishes.

"Geez, Alley, word's all over the bakery about Gracie being in Augusta State."

"People are going to find out, Al. Who told you?" asked Mrs. Alley.

"Nosy Phil Dunn. Actually questioned me about it as we were leaving today."

"None of those Dunns could ever keep to their own business to save their asses."

"I know, Alley, but it's hard to talk about with anyone, you know."

"What did you tell Phil?"

"Told him she needed a special treatment for a blood clot at the base of her brain. Seemed to satisfy him. He went on about how the sweet Gracie he knew couldn't be 'off the deep end.' I know it's just one of many theories old Dr. Bourassa had."

"Who cares? Long as it shuts Phil Dunn up for a while."

"I guess. Well, I'll put Stevie in his crib. Spoiling him rocking him to sleep like this, but the poor little bugger seems to miss his mother so much."

"Baby don't understand what's going on, Al. Waynie misses her, too. We'll get through this somehow, son. We have to."

"Okay, Alley, I'll take your word for it right now. Don't have much else to hold on to presently."

Chapter Nine

What do you suppose this treatment is they keep talking about? Never mind. Just float. Float. Gracie had tried to keep her promise to herself and not talk, for how long she had no idea. At least she thought she had most of the time. May have slipped up once or twice. She couldn't distinguish the days in this place.

Suddenly, a flurry of attendants appeared at Gracie's bed with Miss Downer. Two sturdy, male attendants quickly moved Gracie from her bed to a gurney. Two tight gurney straps kept her from fighting. *Pretend you're in control. Don't act crazy,* Gracie told herself as she gritted her teeth. Ceiling tiles and lights flashed alternately in Gracie's eyes as she was hustled down a long hall. She heard a disquieting moaning sound. She looked sideways and saw a young man rocking back and forth in a chair as he muttered to himself. His refrain was, "No, no, no, no..." She could still hear him faintly as her gurney was suddenly turned into a room filled with odd equipment. She looked around and noticed both Dr. Getchell and Dr. Knowles. It was all she could do to keep herself from speaking up and asking what was happening.

She didn't have much time to think as she was quickly muted by what seemed like a thick rubber bit in her mouth. Something metal was placed firmly on her temples. The people in the room were buzzing around her as fear overtook her. She started to shake and mutter ever so slightly. That was the last thing she remembered before a searing pain overwhelmed her and her whole body convulsed. Black.

Gracie woke up and felt nothing but pain. *What has happened to me?* She struggled to comprehend it. She felt as if she had been trampled by a large crowd.

"Gracie, are you awake finally?" asked someone.

Gracie looked up and sighed as she saw once again Miss Downer's face. She turned away.

"Gracie, please start responding," cooed the young nurse.

"What the Christ did they just do to me?" hissed Gracie.

"My, my. Well, at least you're finally really talking, Gracie," said Miss Downer. "The doctors gave you your first treatment. How do you feel?"

"Like hell. What in God's name kind of treatment is that, anyway?"

"Electroshock treatment, dear. It is intended to rattle you out of that awful depression you have been in. You'll feel better. Are you hungry?"

"How long have I been out?"

"A few hours. That's normal. Nothing to worry about."

Jesus, thought Gracie, *nothing to worry about? Has this fool had this done to her?*

"Gracie, you need to start eating and get your strength back. I'll go get you a tray."

Gracie let Miss Downer feed her some oatmeal. It was very hard to swallow. All of this was very hard to swallow. Gracie couldn't understand why the Good Lord hadn't just let her slip away when she wanted to. She tried to explain this to Dr. Getchell the next day at her first official session, which much to her chagrin was with him instead of the older doctor.

"I don't want to be here or anywhere, damn it all to hell!" cussed Gracie at the doctor.

"Now, Gracie, is that any way for you to talk? Tell me why life is so bad. Where would you like to start?" asked the doctor.

"Dead, that's where I'd like to end. And right now, thank you," replied Gracie.

"Start telling me about your life, Gracie. Start anywhere you would like to," Dr. Getchell said, as he glanced down and flipped through papers on his desk instead of looking at his patient.

"I don't have anything to tell you. I just don't want to live anymore. That's all! By the way, which one of you is actually my doctor?"

"We'll all try to help you here, but we can't if you don't start telling us what is on your mind."

The next few minutes dragged on for both Gracie and Dr. Getchell. Although the doctor made several overtures, Gracie would do nothing but protest about being alive. He finally dismissed her.

Chapter Ten

The Bassett Road in Winslow, Maine was lined with post-WWII, three-room houses. Houses designed for young families just starting out. Tiny boxes with even tinier, wooden rectangles hiding behind trees in the backyards to compensate for a lack of indoor plumbing. Kitchen sinks nicely supplied by cisterns on the roofs. Albert's bakery truck looked too large for the house as it sat in the gravel driveway of Gracie's and his house in this neighborhood. It was on a dirt road. Shortcut between Route 30 and 100. Young families all around, but Albert felt cheated. His little home had been thrown into chaos by Gracie's illness, which he did not understand.

"Al, excuse me. How's Gracie?" Stella asked that early evening as Albert was hustling a box of clothes for the boys to his truck. Childless, beautiful Stella lived next door and had walked over to Albert's driveway.

"Oh, she's doing better," replied Albert. He continued to look busy packing the box.

"When will she be able to return? We all miss her at coffee gatherings."

"Well, Stella, she's better, but it will be a while before she's back here, I'm afraid. When she's out of the hospital, she'll probably stay in town with our friends the Alleys until she gets her sea legs under her. She'll need help with the boys, too. This blood clot business really knocked her around."

"Heavens, I had never heard of such a thing until you told us about it. Can't imagine it. No wonder Gracie looked so pale and sick."

Stella had been walking over into Albert's yard as they spoke. Suddenly, she was close enough to reach out and pat Albert's left forearm. He jumped slightly.

"Al, you'll let me know if I can help you with anything, won't you?"

Albert gazed at Stella. He didn't know what to say. He blushed.

"Oh, Al, don't be silly. I'm talking about a meal or mending the boys' clothes, or something like that."

"Oh." Albert looked down and kicked a rock.

"Or anything you need. Bye now. Say hi to Gracie for me."

Stella turned and walked back toward her house. Albert watched her and felt a bit ashamed of the visceral reaction he was having while looking at her backside walking away.

Chapter Eleven

"Over four thousand patients in this hellhole and only one doctor and a couple interns!" fussed Dr. Ken Knowles to himself. He told his wife they should not have moved to Central Maine, free house or not. His in-laws had died within six months of one another about five years ago and left them an old ark of a house in Gardiner. It was magnificent when a paper baron had built it over a hundred years ago. Unfortunately, many owners later, it was at present a capacious, handyman's special. Now here he sat with stacks of patient files on his huge, oak desk in this bland office of Augusta State Hospital. The only nice thing about the room was its view of the Kennebec River out of the one window. Taking this job here was a mistake. The two interns he finally convinced the administration to bring on staff were some help, but one was a slippery young man. Couldn't be trusted. The place had lovely nurses, but the orderlies! Some of them were sadistic buggers; he knew it. A soft knock on his office door made Knowles stop his agonizing.

"Yes?" he barked. No reply.

"My life for a secretary in this public institution. For heaven's sake," the doctor grumbled as he walked over and opened the door. He discovered a small female patient standing outside his office. Her head was bowed. "What do you need, dear? Where's your ward nurse?"

The frail young woman said nothing. She didn't raise her head.

"Darn it all, are you Grace?"

The little creature managed to nod while still keeping her head down.

"I'm sorry. I had an appointment with you, didn't I? Come in, come in. I have no secretary in this damned place." He paused and looked over at the patient. She stood just inside the door. He watched her for a minute. Drowning in a hospital gown and over-jacket, the tiny thing had tiny feet in slippers too big for them. Stringy, chestnut-brown hair. He couldn't see her face with her head held so low. Then he remembered he'd already had an encounter with her and had talked to her husband about electroshock therapy when Dr. Getchell had neglected to do so just before treatment had been scheduled. Twenty-three-year old. Arrived catatonic in a strait jacket a month ago. Suicidal. The doctor suddenly remembered that scene. Records told him she was partway through a series of electroshock therapy treatments. Had refused several times to say much of anything to Dr. Getchell. Not that he could blame her for that.

"Well, for heaven's sake now, sit down over here," said Dr. Knowles, patting his hair down with one hand while using the other to point to a huge wooden chair. He circled around his desk to sit down. "How are you doing?" No answer. "Grace? Do you prefer Gracie? That's what I seem to remember. Gracie, can you talk to me?"

"I need to go home to care of my boys. I'll be good," whispered Gracie without looking up from her rigid, hunched-over position on the very edge of the chair in front of Knowles' desk.

"You have young boys at home?"

"Waynie and Stevie," she said, glancing quickly at the doctor before looking back down.

"I see. Well, I'm sure they miss you."

"They'll be taken if I don't get home. Like my siblings years ago, you see. They do that. I can't let that happen," Gracie said with a bit more force in her voice. She started to rock back and forth.

"You lost siblings?"

"State took them when I was a baby."

"They didn't take you?"

"No. No one's ever wanted me."

"How about your husband?"

Gracie grumbled and bowed her head even lower. "It's okay. Don't trust no one."

"Is that why you wanted to leave this world, Gracie?"

Gracie looked up. "I'll be good now. I'll take care of my boys and my house. I need to go home!" She studied the floor again.

"Gracie, have you ever had anyone you trusted?"

Gracie rustled in the chair she could have fit four of herself in. She looked out the window that didn't have a thick wire screen like the ones in the ward. She appeared to have no answer. Dr. Knowles just smiled and chewed on the tip of his glasses bow. Age had taught him to be patient. He didn't want to scare this little creature into silence again. When he looked away for a minute and then back, he noticed Gracie was studying him with large, childlike blue eyes. Her left cheek had a nasty, jagged scar. She immediately put her hand to her face and looked down.

They sat quietly for a few more minutes. "Had one person," Gracie finally said.

"Yes, can you tell me more?"

Gracie looked out the window again and let out a small laugh. "Jackknife Fred. He cared about me."

"Jackknife Fred? What a name!"

Silence filled the office as Gracie peered out the window while occasionally glancing at the doctor. Then the story of her childhood friend began to pour out of her.

"Jackknife Fred lived in a shack behind our house in Windsor when I was a kid. Don't know why he did. Our house weren't much more 'n his. I used to go around to the back of our house and run up the path to his place and bug him." Gracie suddenly grinned. "Jackknife and I both had scars, see…Jackknife Fred's scar had always mystified me. It started at the left corner of his mouth, just missing the outer edge of his lips. It ran diagonally over his left cheek to the top of his neck, below his ear, and then shot immediately down toward his shoulder. Usually a shirt collar stopped the study of this fascinating mark, but that day it was different. Jackknife was busy digging a hole behind his shack when I startled him. His shirt lay in a heap behind him.

I said to him, 'Hey, Jackknife! Lordy, I never realized that goddamned scar of yours went right down to almost your belly button! Heavens!' I stood and admired the line on my favorite neighbor.

Jackknife says something to me like, 'Jesus Christ, Miss Murray, you startled me half to death. Don't you know better than to sneak up on a man like that? You might be sporting a scar yourself, by God.'

'Already got me a scar, so there!' I stuck out my left cheek to him with my tongue jammed in it to fully emphasize the mark.

'So you do. Can't remember when that happened. Remind me.'

'First off, call me Gracie,' I told him that day.

'I may live in this old shack, but I do have manners,' says Jackknife to me. 'I'll call you Gracie if I have your permission.'

'You and me should be on a first name basis, Jackknife. We're good friends.'

'All right, Gracie,' he tells me. 'Don't be telling your mother about this friendship, though. Now, what are you doing back here pestering the likes of me? You here to tell me about your scar?'

'Remember I got this scar a couple years ago when the Brann's damned German Shepard attacked me? 'Member, I was eight. Ma couldn't make enough milk for Ira John, and I went by the dog's yard to pick up a pail of goat's milk.' Ira John's my baby brother, you see, Doc.

'Jesus, I do remember when you got mangled like that. Damned dog was a menace. So you come up here to talk about scars, did you?' asks Jackknife.

'Oh, no. Ma says I have to find my father. Why, I don't know. I certainly don't miss him, but she seems to think she needs him for something. Jackknife, how did you get your scar? No one seems to know.'

'How 'bout your old man?' Jackknife quizzes me.

'Shit on him," I told Jackknife. "Ma's better off without him. Won't you tell me about that there scar? Please?'

'For heaven's sake, child,' he scolds me.

'Please, with molasses on it?' I begged him.

Jackknife sat down on the pile of dirt he had created with his digging. I plunked down near him.

'First things first, little girl. Your father got in a fight last night at a poker game at Chester Whyte's. Last I saw him, he was sleeping off a few hard whacks to the head he received trying to cheat someone. Well, that and quite a bit of drink in Chester's barn.'

'Ayah, Jackknife. Sounds about right. But how 'bout that scar?'

'I was doing something here, you know. Digging myself a hole for a new outhouse here.'

'Most people just clean out the one they got,' I teased him.

'Well, Gracie, I ain't most people," Jackknife says back to me.

'Ma would agree with you on that!'

'Oh, yeah? Just what does she say about me now?'

'Ain't pretty, Jackknife.'

'Do tell. Tell me anyway, young 'un.'

'Ma calls you a foul-mouthed, shady, poker-playing bastard.'

Jackknife says something like, 'Really?'

'With a heart of gold, though,' I says to him, 'unlike the poker-playing son of a bitch of a drunk she up and married. He takes off for days and don't worry about us starving or freezing to death. She appreciates you bringing firewood and meat, even if it just be squirrel at times.'

Well, that made Jackknife smile, you know. 'Lord, Gracie, you're spending way too much time with folks like me. No amount of soap could wash out that mouth of yours!' he barks.

'Don't care none. You gonna tell me 'bout that scar, or not? That little Christer of a brother of mine is gonna wake up soon from his nap and give Ma trouble. You know Ira John. I don't have all day.'

'Then you best off scoot right now to help with Ira John, Missy.'

'Why won't you tell me?' I begged him again.

'The story of this here damned scar, Gracie, takes a good hour to tell decently.'

'Can I come back tomorrow and have you tell it to me?'

'If I'm here, I'll gladly tell you,' he promised me.

'Promise for sure? Is it the very reason for your name?'

'Tomorrow, Gracie. I think I hear a commotion coming from your way. Maybe you best get along and let a man finish the work he done cut out for hisself.'

I turned and started down the dirt path to my house but then stopped and looked back. 'You'll be seeing me tomorrow, Jackknife.'

'Okay, little one. Don't forget to tell your mother about your old man now.'

'Christ, Jackknife, let's hope he turns into Rip Van Winkle and gives us a good break without him.'"

"But he didn't, Doctor Knowles. My old man came home and wreaked his usual havoc in our house. Ira John and I hid under my bed while he had at my mother. Think he passed out that particular time before he could do her too much harm." Gracie whispered this last line to Dr. Knowles. She suddenly looked embarrassed and started playing with the tie around her waist.

"What a story teller you are!" Dr. Knowles leaned back in his chair. "Do you know what happened to this Jackknife?"

"Nope. Couple years later Ma took really sick, and my little brother and I were taken by relatives. Well, he was snatched up, and I was passed around to whoever would take me. I asked a couple times about Jackknife, but no one thought I should worry about the likes of him."

"I'm sorry, Gracie."

"Well, that's just the way things are with my life. Someone shows a glimmer of caring for me, and I lose them." Gracie looked down at her slippers.

"Can you tell me more, Gracie?"

Gracie sat quietly. "I'm really tired, Doc."

Dr. Knowles waited a couple more minutes and then dismissed her. She left the office like a hummingbird scared away from a red flower blossom, quickly and almost noiselessly. Knowles sat thinking about the vivid childhood recollection he had just heard. He marveled at the poverty and abuse some of these poor, rural patients had suffered. He opened Grace's file again and glanced over the first page that talked about her relatives. Her father had spent time there in that hospital in 1923, a year before she was born. Diagnosis: habitual drunkard. And yet he had spawned an obviously bright little storyteller like Grace.

Chapter Twelve

"Johnny, I don't know how long your sister'll be in the hospital. I just don't know, I tell ya." Albert rearranged his belt on his sagging green work pants for the second time in just a couple minutes.

"Jesus, Al, what are they going to do to her in there? You know Aunt Edie won't even talk to me about it. Acts like it isn't even happening. Starts mumbling prayers when I press her 'bout it," said Johnny. "I want to go see her, dammit."

"Can't. You're underage."

"Horseshit! I'll lie about my age. I'll tell 'em I'm eighteen."

Albert laughed. "God, Ira John Murray, you don't even look your actual age of fifteen!"

"Christ, I know. Damned Murray short-man problems."

"And baby face to boot!"

Now they both chuckled. As they stood in the yard of the Bassett Road house where they had met that afternoon, a woman pretended to be busy sweeping her front steps next door.

"Stella still acting too interested in you, Al?" chuckled Johnny.

"Knew I shouldn't of told the likes of you about that," answered Albert. He waved at Stella.

"Come over to Alley's with me and sponge a free supper and see the boys. They miss you."

"Gotta hitch myself back to Windsor, Al."

"I'll drive you after supper, kid. Could use a dose of Aunt Edie right now."

They jumped in the bakery truck.

"How can you ride around in this thing without eating donuts all the time? Is there anything left over back there, Al?" Johnny was twisted around in the passenger seat, foraging through the closest shelves as they bumped along the Bassett Road. "Bingo! Chocolate sugared. My favorites!"

"Knock yourself out, kid." Albert shook his head. "I get so I can't stand the smell of them, say nothing of eat them. Don't eat too many. Alley will try to stuff you with supper, and you'll get sick."

"I like that old lady, Al," mumbled Johnny through a mouthful of donut. "She's a funny little thing, but I do. She don't go scolding or preaching gospel to me every time she sees me."

"Probably would like to but figures it wouldn't do any good. She's smart. I can't badmouth her none. She's been my salvation through this whole thing with your sister."

Johnny chewed for a minute and swallowed loudly. He turned to Albert and said, "I got something I need to ask you about. I overheard Aunt Edie telling Uncie about Gracie's behavior just before you took her to Alley's for help."

"What'd you hear?"

"Edie told Uncie that Gracie was playing with your rifle. Said the neighbors called you at work about coming to take it away from her out on your front lawn."

"What?"

"Don't give me no shit, Al. You know Bunny Cates across the street from you loves me. While I was waiting on the front steps for you this afternoon, she came tromping over to say hi. She verified the whole story. Tells me Gracie has been acting weird as all get out."

"Well, Christ, Johnny, what do you want me to say? Why do you think I finally took her to that hospital in Augusta? Do you think I wanted to?"

"She tried to jump out a window at Alley's, didn't she?"

"Tried? Jesus, she did! It's a wonder she didn't really hurt herself bad. Early in the morning the day Alley and I took her down to Augusta."

"Why didn't you tell me, Al?"

"Because she's your sister, and you're just a kid, dammit!"

Both Albert and Johnny leaned against their respective doors now. Albert gazed at the road.

Johnny stuck his head out the side window and caught air like a dog.

Albert broke the silence. "Listen, Johnny, you can't be mad at me. I have enough people pissed at me as it is. Please understand I'm going through some shit here."

Johnny pulled his head into the truck. "I know. I know, Al. Just don't keep me in the dark anymore. I love my sister, but I know she's been acting crazy. Last time I visited and you were at work, she started telling me all about a vacuum cleaner salesman who's out to get her. Then she proceeded to tell me things would have been better if she hadn't had Stevie. Why would she be blaming things on the baby, for God's sake?"

"I don't know, Johnny. Lord, her story about that salesman. And she started getting so angry with the baby. I don't have any idea what's going on with her at this point. Scares the hell out of me."

"Me, too, Al. Me, too."

The ride to Alley's was finished in silence.

Later that night, after returning to Alley's from dropping Johnny off at Aunt Edie's house and passing pleasantries with her and Uncie, instead of brooding about not being able to sleep Albert thought about his conversation with Johnny. He had been so pleased to father two children in less than two years, and not just any children, but boys; big, healthy baby boys who seemed to love him as much as he loved them. In high school while in a fight—the Scottish boys versus the dark-skinned teens in Lebanese Town down in Waterville—he had been violently kicked in the groin. His left testicle was driven up into his body. His family didn't spend money on doctors frivolously, so his injury went unattended. He always wondered if this would affect his ability to be a dad. It hadn't.

He couldn't understand why his young wife wasn't thrilled with two boys who were seventeen months apart. She fussed about changing diapers and lost weight trying to nurse the younger one, but wasn't that a mother's duty? She seemed so depressed when he got home from work each day. Cussed at him about not pulling out of her before finishing, as he had done before their wedding. They were married now, he had told her, but he still tried to most of the time after the first baby, although it didn't work. He tried, but he was actually fertile, much to his enjoyment.

And then came the day he found her with his hunting rifle for a second time. She was passed out on the kitchen floor. He checked for spent shells, and not finding any, went looking for his baby boys. He found them both sitting in Steve's crib. Huddled together. He couldn't fathom how such babies knew trouble was brewing, but they seemed to. It was then, after making sure they were okay, that he went back down and packed them all in his baker's truck and drove to Alley's house for help.

Thank God Johnny didn't know about that second episode with the gun. Bunny Cates hadn't found out about that one. Sleep overcame Albert as he once again mulled over what his young brother-in-law might or might not know.

Chapter Thirteen

As Gracie walked back to the ward one day, she was amazed that the 'powers that be' let her wander on her own after just recently keeping her tied down like a wild animal. She saw a blonde woman sitting in a chair in the hall in front of her. It was the same woman who had caught her eye a couple of times in the ward recently. Gracie stopped at her chair and looked down at her without saying a word.

The woman looked up. "I'm okay, I'm okay," the patient fussed up at Gracie. Gracie noticed that she was brushing away tears from her face.

"Sure you're all right?" asked Gracie.

"Of course, of course," repeated the woman. "Don't tell, please don't tell! Don't tell anyone about Dr. Getchell. It's my fault."

"What are you talking about? And why in the world are your clothes all unbuttoned like that?"

"It's my own fault. That's what Miss Downer tells me."

"What is?"

"Do you have therapy with Dr. Getchell?"

"I refuse to talk with that guy. Why?"

"Oh, good for you. Try to avoid him. By the way, I'm Cheryl Lee. What's your name?"

"Gracie, but…"

"Gracie, please don't tell about my crying and all. Please don't. Okay?"

'Therapy' in the form of shock treatments continued for three weeks for Gracie. She rather enjoyed having Cheryl Lee as a shadow for company. They often sat in silence in the ward or on a bench in the hall. Gracie did most of the talking. Cheryl Lee was shy. "I'll be damned lucky if my brain will even work after all this shit," Gracie announced to Cheryl Lee as they sat looking out a large window that framed the side grounds of the hospital.

"There are worse things than that, Gracie," said Cheryl Lee.

"I don't know what it would be! You suppose the Nazis used it for torture in the war?"

"Who?"

"The Nazis, the Germans."

Cheryl Lee looked at Gracie with wide eyes.

"Good Christ, Cheryl Lee, how long have you been here?"

"I can't really remember, Gracie. I think I came here in what would have been my junior year in high school. Not sure, but I think so. Yes, my junior year."

"When were you to graduate?"

"1939, class of '39. I'm a Lawrence High Bulldog, I am."

Gracie just smiled at her friend. *Heavens,* thought Gracie, *this poor thing has been here almost a decade.* She didn't try to explain the Nazis or anything like that to her. She grabbed Cheryl Lee's hand. Cheryl smiled and put her head on Gracie's shoulder. They sat there.

Gracie was unaware of how much time had passed. She heard someone scurrying down the hall just beyond them. Before she could guess who it might be, Nurse Downer was pausing in front of them.

"There you are, Gracie. I've been looking everywhere for you," said Miss Downer.

"I don't have many places to hide," said Gracie still sitting with Cheryl's head on her shoulder.

"Oh, Gracie, how can someone with such a wonderful sense of humor have problems like you do? I just don't know."

"The Lord works in mysterious ways, Nurse Downer," replied Gracie. Gracie thought but didn't say: *How is it possible that you have the brains to find the hospital every morning, Nurse Downer?*

"Oh, Gracie, you are funny! Dr. Knowles needs to see you right away. I think he might have really good news for you, dear."

"They're planning to get me a pony for my twenty-fourth birthday?"

"Gracie! The news has something to do with that handsome hubby of yours."

"How do you know about Albert?"

"We know all kinds of things about you, dear, but right now you need to be running to Dr. Knowles' office. Lickity split, Gracie!"

"Gracie, I didn't know you were married!" said Cheryl Lee sitting up and looking at Gracie.

Gracie looked away from both Cheryl Lee and Nurse Downer. *Where has this asshole of a husband been all this time?* She couldn't move. She sat rigidly and stared at the floor.

"Gracie, please don't let this news of the outside world upset you like this. Come now. I'll walk with you down to his office. Gracie, please!" said Miss Downer.

Miss Downer reached down and touched Gracie's right forearm. Cheryl Lee moved away from them.

Gracie walked down the hall with Nurse Downer. She said nothing. When they reached Dr. Knowles' office, she was surprised to look around and notice the doctor wasn't there. She had no reaction to her husband.

"Gracie?" said Albert as he got up from a chair.

"I need to go home. Need to take care of the boys. I'll be good now," said Gracie to her husband.

"Gracie, I can't take you home just yet, but the doctor says you're doing better now. How are you feeling?" asked Albert.

"How the Christ do you think I'm feeling!" yelled Gracie back at him.

"Gracie! Now that is no way to speak to your husband. He's here to visit with you," chided Nurse Downer.

"You can shut up!" replied Gracie.

"What?" asked Miss Downer.

Albert reached out and cuffed Gracie on her right cheek and then immediately cringed and looked down. "You can't talk to them like this! I'll never be able to get you out of here if you act like this. Please, Gracie!"

Gracie said nothing. Miss Downer grabbed her arm and started pulling her toward the office door. "I'm afraid this was too soon to visit, Mr. Grant."

"Wait, I'm sorry, please. I'm just so upset with all this," said Albert as he watched his wife and the nurse go quickly out the door.

"Call the doctor for another appointment a little later in the month," replied the nurse over her shoulder. Gracie never looked back at him.

Chapter Fourteen

Dr. Knowles burst into the nurses' station like a vengeful father. "Who the hell told Albert Grant that it was okay to visit his wife?" The four nurses present were silent. They didn't even dare peek at one another. Nurse Downer put a patient chart down on the counter, looked at the silver-haired doctor and bit her lower lip.

"Poor Mr. Grant called the station here a couple days ago, Dr. Knowles. He sounded so pathetic," Miss Downer said while looking around for support from her fellow nurses. When none was offered, she continued, "You were not in the building, so I found Dr. Getchell and asked him about Mr. Grant having a brief visit. He thought it might actually help Grace. So did I, Dr. Knowles. We had no idea she would have such an angry reaction to seeing her adorable little husband. He's so sweet, and we figured…"

"You and Dr. Getchell, the resident charmer. I see. Do you have any idea how long it took me to gain any rapport with Grace? Was adorable little Dr. Getchell able to get anywhere with her when he tried?"

Nurse Downer stood looking at the doctor with her mouth open. The other nurses had turned away from him. One tried to sneak away but was caught by Nurse Wight, who faced the male intruder with, "Dr. Knowles, they can hear you hollering in the ward. You're going to upset the patients. Please tell my nurses here what you want in a reasonable tone of voice or leave."

"What I want, my dear Mrs. Wight, is some respect as far as consulting me before allowing visitations of my patients."

"Is that all, Dr. Knowles?"

"No; no it isn't. I do not want any of your nurses to consult Dr. Getchell in my absence."

"Then you shall have just that, Doctor. Are any of you unclear about the doctor's demands?" she asked the young nurses. Silence.

"We have heard you and understand you. Is there anything else, Dr. Knowles?"

Knowles glared at Wight for a few seconds then turned and left, all the while muttering profanities under his breath.

"Oh, Mrs. Wight, you saved us!" Miss Downer blathered. She and the other young nurses started giggling.

"I just wish I could save all of you from Dr. Getchell," announced Mrs. Wight. "Now get to work, all of you!" She stomped out, swearing under her breath, too.

Chapter Fifteen

I don't even have my Tippy to pet. Albert was wallowing in self-pity on the side steps of his Basset Road home. He'd had to drive his dog up to Livermore to his sister's farm when his young family was forced to move in town for help. Alley had done enough for him without asking her to put up with a dog, but did he ever miss his pooch. His presence was almost palpable here at this little house; the house that had been purchased to set things right for Gracie. She had never forgiven him for selling the other house he had built for them in Benton on his parents' side yard. He sold it in order to save his father's farm. Gracie stood and sobbed as the people who had purchased the little structure took it away on skidders. Now he was the only one who stopped at the Basset Road house. He and some of the other men in the neighborhood called it the 'Bastard Road.' He grinned as that thought crossed his mind, but somehow it made Albert feel better to spend a little time here at the end of his bread route before he journeyed back to Alley's and his boys.

It was a very warm October day. Indian summer, Mainers called it. Albert felt his undershirt cling to his chest and armpits as he flapped his untucked Harris Bakery shirt. *Stupid uniform's always been too big, but now I look like a clown in it with the weight I've lost. It's too much. Just too much. What the hell is dementia praecox anyway? The catatonic type to boot! They're going to cure her somehow with electric shocks? What will come home to me after that, if she comes home at all?*

Albert tried to remember the last time he had dared to touch Gracie in an affectionate way. He couldn't. Seemed like she had been too fragile for a long time. Her sister Flippie had scolded him about how thin Gracie was when she visited a couple months ago. He'd told her he didn't know what to do, and she was no help. Everyone was full of criticism, but no one had good advice. Maybe except for dear, old Alley. She had jumped in with both feet and tried the best she could until it got to be too much for her, too.

Albert felt so alone. *Maybe it isn't just Tippy I miss here today.* He thought about the woman on his bakery route who had grabbed the bread placard out of her front window just this morning and grinned at him while explaining she could use more than just a loaf or two of bread.

"Pies, too?" Albert had quipped with a knowing grin.

"Oh, you handsome young thing! I could show you how to make a great homemade pie and then some," replied the customer, who had to be almost old enough to be his mother.

"Got to get going now," he'd replied with a quick glance at the customer's shapely housedress. She may have been close to his mother's age, but she certainly wasn't built like Mother Grant. Sitting now on his steps, Albert laughed out loud.

"What are you finding so funny here all by yourself, Al?" asked a sweet-toned voice.

"Stella! I didn't hear you coming," said Albert, standing up quickly and tucking in his shirt.

"You were so lost in thought just now, Al, a herd of elephants could have snuck up on you. What are you doing here?"

"Just thinking, Stel. Missing Tippy-dog and mulling over things that have been happening. You want to hear the latest about Gracie, I suppose."

"I'll listen to that, but I really want to talk about you. Somehow, you're lost in the middle of this mess, Al. Wish I could do something for you." Stella reached up with her right hand and gently brushed the side of Albert's face. The same hand found a spot to rest on at his heart.

He went to grab her hand, but at the same time she slipped down into his arms. He hugged her as they sat on the steps together now. Keeping her in his arms, he started to cry. She let him for a few minutes.

"Al, you need to think about yourself every once in a while, you know," Stella whispered. "You won't do anyone any good if you collapse, too."

"Don't have time to think about myself. Too busy trying to hold things together as it is."

Stella held him tightly now.

"Stella, what if someone sees us like this?" asked Albert as he pulled back slightly.

"I don't really care. Let them talk. So many gossips on this dreary little side road. It would make their day." She pulled him back into a warm hug. Albert didn't take it any further, but he didn't fight her off. He felt so good in her arms.

Chapter Sixteen

Somehow Gracie felt quite comfortable in Dr. Knowles' disheveled office. Stacks of folders stood up from the worn wooden floor all around the chair she occupied during her sessions with him. His desk was an untidy hodgepodge of letters and notebooks. As he peered over them to look at her that day, she asked him, "Why am I here?"

"What do you mean, Gracie?" asked the doctor.

"I don't belong here. I've told you the patients in my ward act really weird. Something is wrong with them."

"Really; so do you remember how you felt when you arrived a month ago?"

"What do you mean?"

Dr. Knowles looked at Gracie and smiled. "Never mind. Let's talk about why you were so angry when you saw your husband."

Gracie pulled her knees up to her chest and turned away from Dr. Knowles. She stared at the floor for several minutes and then whispered, "His visit surprised me. Poor thing can't begin to understand me. Nobody does really."

"What do you mean, Gracie?"

Gracie put her legs down and looked at the doctor. "Okay, Dr. Knowles, okay; so nobody understands what I've put up with marrying into that Grant family. I was stuck on an old chicken farm that wasn't making any money. My husband catered to his parents as if he weren't married with a baby boy and a too-soon pregnant-again wife. Albert started building our own house on the side field, and then I watched the shell of it go down the road on skidders. Sold to pay on a delinquent mortgage of a homestead that didn't even belong to us. My mother-in-law, who wouldn't say shit if she had a mouthful, had the gall to ask me why I had gotten pregnant again so soon after Wayne since we couldn't afford the first one. Think she would consider explaining to her son that withdrawal doesn't work? Lifting bales of hay out in the barn doesn't cause a miscarriage either, much to my chagrin. Even tried to lose the baby by throwing myself down a set of stairs. At least that shut up Al's mother for a while. Old man Grant, old A.R., was a tyrant! Old Arthur Russell would yell 'shit,' and my husband would squat and strain. I'm glad the old bastard died. I am. So there!"

Gracie stopped talking suddenly and looked frightened. "Don't write that down, doctor. Please don't."

"I don't really write down what you say, Gracie. Can't take short hand or write fast. Why are you so worried?"

"Oh, I worry that you'll think I'm bad. Was I really bad when I first came?"

"I don't think you're bad, Gracie. I just want to help you."

"Did I act crazy like some of those other ward patients?"

Dr. Knowles hesitated for a minute. "You seemed very confused, but I saw something in you that made me believe we could help you. You're better already."

"I'd like to believe that." Gracie looked out the window again in silence.

"Gracie, do you want to talk anymore?"

"I'm really tired. Can I go?" Gracie's voice sounded like a child's again.

Dr. Knowles nodded.

Chapter Seventeen

Flowers, thought Albert, *dear French Lucy loves her flowers.* Every wall in the Winslow farmhouse where Gracie stayed from the time she was twelve was covered with flowered wallpaper. Billowy, blossom-printed drapes dwarfed every window. And the colors! Purples blended with different shades of red, along with other bright tints. Nothing like the drab house Albert's mother had kept in Benton. He sat opposite Gracie's Uncle Polly while waiting for Polly's wife Lucy to bring in a tray of tea. This maternal uncle of Gracie's had the given name of William. Albert always chuckled about how someone with a royal name like that put up with the nickname Polly. He had always been a puzzle to Albert in many ways. Albert knew Polly and his wife didn't care for him, and they only had one purpose for insisting that he pay them a visit this afternoon. Albert felt anxious in this house today, as he usually did.

"Where are the girls?" asked Albert after a long period of silence.

"Darned if I know," replied Polly.

"Polly, they're upstairs doing homework and not to hear this conversation about Gracie. You know that," snapped Lucy as she entered the room and placed a laden tray down on the coffee table between Albert and Polly. Then she hopped up slightly and plopped herself down on the couch next to Polly, who did not respond to being bounced in the air. Now, Polly was small like the other men in the family, but Lucy was a creature to behold. At four foot nine, she was about as broad as she was tall. Gracie always told Albert that this uncle and his wife had treated her like a maid from the time she started staying with them, but she still was oddly attached to them. He felt he had to be careful with what he said here.

"Albert, we want to know what happened to our Gracie," announced Lucy without any moves toward the tea. "She was a beautiful, smart girl when she was with us, wasn't she, Polly?"

"What, dear?" Polly asked.

Lucy never bothered to clarify her comments for her husband. Instead she asked Albert, "Just what has been going on in your household, young man? What caused our Gracie to be this sick?"

Albert would've loved to be able to say that he treated her better than they did, but he didn't. "Our family doctor over town, you know Dr. Bourassa, thinks it could have something to do with Stevie's birth. Sometimes women go through a blue period after the birth of a baby, particularly a second one soon after the first. She got really run down."

"She should have had some help, Al. Those babies were close together. Never been that strong, our Gracie," said Lucy. Now she started fooling with the tea cups.

Albert looked away. He knew Gracie wouldn't want him to alienate these folks. She could criticize them all day, but she never allowed Albert to say a negative word about them. He glanced back at them. Both Lucy and Polly were staring at him with pleading expressions. Maybe they felt guilty about working her so hard. Maybe this was the reason they demanded an explanation from him, so he gave them one. "Dr. Bourassa also has a theory about a blood clot at the base of Gracie's brain. Thinks it could be causing the erratic behavior. Maybe the shock treatments will loosen it."

"Never heard of such a thing," said Lucy. "Say something Polly. She's your niece, for heaven's sake."

Silence stood between them for a couple of moments, and then Polly said, "Lucy, we don't know what is happening. We can blame Al all we want for this, but it won't do any good. Let's just tell him what we want."

Now Albert shifted in his seat. "What are you talking about?"

"Hospital refuses to let us go see Gracie. Say we're not immediate family. We need you to explain Gracie's situation, so they'll let us visit." Polly was now sitting up straight and giving Albert a commanding look that he'd never seen from him before.

"You really want to visit? It's not a pleasant place, you know," replied Albert.

"Al, we need to see our Gracie. Will you give us permission, or not?" said Polly. Lucy sat next to her husband giving him a look of admiration now. The tea was still unserved.

"I guess I could do that. She might appreciate a visit from you." Albert had been expecting a slew of accusations from these two instead of this.

"You have to sign some papers saying we can visit. Do it when you can, please."

"I will. I need to get back to the boys soon," Albert said, glancing at the molasses cookies on the tea tray.

"Thanks, Al," said Lucy with her hands folded in her lap. She and Polly stared at Albert across the coffee table. Albert finally stood up and started making his way into the kitchen toward the back door. His hosts stood up and watched him leave. Nothing had been asked about how he or his baby boys were doing.

The empty bakery truck made Albert feel even more alone as he sat for a moment thinking before starting the engine and taking off from the farm. His gloom was broken by a gentle rap on his truck window. A familiar face was peeking through the glass at him. Horn-rimmed glasses and a serious expression. Twelve-year-old Shirley, third daughter of Polly and Lucy; Albert's favorite of the four girls. He rolled the window down and smiled at her.

"Is she going to be okay?" asked Shirl.

"What do you know about it?" asked Albert, not sure what to divulge.

"I know she's in the hospital. I heard Mom and Pa talking. Gracie looked poorly all summer, for goodness sake. I'm not foolish."

"Oh, I see. She'll be okay."

"You just telling me this?"

"No, I've been told by her doctor she's getting better."

"What's the doctor's name?"

"Dr. Knowles. What difference does that make to you?"

"Just worried about her, you know. How's the boys?"

"Okay. Thanks for asking."

"You look awful skinny."

"I could have used some of your mother's molasses cookies, I guess."

"You didn't get one with your tea?"

"Didn't get tea. Wasn't an extremely pleasant visit."

"Wait here."

Shirl disappeared inside the house through the back door. When she returned, she had something wrapped in a worn dish towel. She put her left index finger to her mouth in a shushing motion as she passed the bundle to Albert with her right hand. Then she backed away from the truck, glancing toward the house.

"I'll say hi to Gracie for you next time I visit, Shirl. Thanks!"

Chapter Eighteen

Gracie found that cooperating in her therapy with Dr. Knowles worked to her advantage. After a few sessions with him, she earned the privilege of walking around outside without a hospital guard, so she decided to take full advantage of it. As she walked out the front door of the building she had been held in for what seemed like forever, she remembered it was fall. She also remembered her twenty-fourth birthday was coming soon. She smiled as she stood on the hill overlooking the Kennebec River and downtown Augusta on the opposite side. She was startled to see how many buildings were part of the hospital. As she walked down a path lined by bright orange maple trees, she felt the chill of fall and wished she had a sweater on instead of the baggy hospital jacket, but she wasn't cold enough to turn back. It was so easy on a day like this to pretend she was somewhere else.

The first building she paused to look at was huge and white. Greek revival columns flanked the large double doors on the front of it. She almost went up the steps to the ornate door, but she decided to stay outdoors. The air was so wonderful. Walking on toward other buildings, she suddenly felt a feeling of déjà vu. She knew she had been in this spot before. Then she remembered the discussion of her Aunt Bernice selling her house and land to the hospital. The huge campus must have swallowed up her place as one of its many buildings. She wanted to find it.

"That's it!" she said out loud to herself. She was in front of an old wood-framed house jerry-rigged with the accoutrements necessary to turn it into an office building. She noticed signs were screwed on the siding without attention to balance or eye-pleasing placement. Iron hand rails ran alongside the old original wooden rails that now leaned over too far for safety. She was horrified by the looks of the fire escape that broke out on the side of the building. Then she was awash in memories. She went up the steps and through the front door. She peeked in one room.

"Miss, where are you supposed to be?" asked a secretary looking up from her typewriter. Gracie didn't stop. She continued to take in her surroundings. The immense parlor was lacking its dark furniture that Aunt Bernice had in there. French doors leading into the dining room had disappeared. Gracie closed her eyes and could still picture the colorful, picture-patterned wallpaper of the room.

"Miss, I asked you where you were supposed to be. Did you hear me?"

"This is my Aunt Bernice's house," said Gracie.

"What?"

"My Aunt Bernice's."

"What are you talking about, child?"

"My Aunt Bernice lived here. I was only inside once, though. We were the poor relations who were only allowed 'door yard visits,' mind you." Gracie remembered how humiliated her mother was years ago as she stood there at the back door of this elegant house with Gracie and Ira John, who'd kept pestering her with questions about why they weren't allowed to go in and visit. Her little brother Ira John had announced he was tired and hungry. Aunt Bernice's maid handed them a bag of groceries through the door as she herself said a curt goodbye. The three poor relatives sat on the outer edge of the large lawn and ate some of the food from the bag. At least Ira John and Gracie ate. Gracie now remembered her mother hadn't. She had just sat quietly and stared back at the house. Gracie wondered what her dear mother had been thinking that day. Her reverie was broken by the secretary's voice.

"Helen, Helen! We have a visitor. Please call for an attendant or two."

Gracie touched the trim of the doorway and whispered, "Oh, I remember standing at this door and marveling over this fancy wood.

Aunt Bernice hollered at me, 'Child, don't touch anything with those filthy hands of yours!'"

"Dear, what ward are you from? What is your name?"

"Oh, I'm Gracie, but I was talking about my aunt, you see." It was then that Gracie took a good look at the secretary. "My aunt lived here. That is what I'm trying to tell you."

A second secretary appeared in the side door. "Do we think she could be dangerous?"

"They usually don't let them wander if they are. Have you called for help?" asked the first secretary. The request was met with a nod, and both ladies stood peering at Gracie now.

"You don't understand. I was taking a walk, and I remembered about my aunt and decided to come in and take a peek," said Gracie. "I'm just looking. Please don't call anyone."

"Right, right," said the first secretary. "Your aunt lived here."

"You think they will send someone over right away?" asked the other secretary.

"Please don't! I am okay!" Gracie looked around for the door. She started toward it when it opened abruptly in front of her. Two white-jacketed men came in.

"Hope you brought a straitjacket with you. This little darling think she's visiting some Aunt Bernice, for heaven sakes!" said the first secretary.

Gracie crouched against a file cabinet and covered herself with her arms. The two orderlies grabbed her from both sides. Gracie felt a sting at her upper left arm.

"What do you think you're doing here?" The words of Dr. Knowles pierced Gracie's ears as she came out of the fog she'd been floating in. She tried to rub her face. She couldn't; she realize she was straitjacketed again and felt panic, shame, anger, and frustration all in one fell swoop. She noticed she was back in the hall of Ward 5.

"Well, Dr. Knowles, we got a call, see…"

"This patient is allowed freedom on the campus. Did anyone question her before jabbing her and slapping her in this damned jacket?"

"No, Doc, but the ladies over at the central office called and said she wandered into their office and acted as if she had screws loose, and…"

"Why didn't one of you question her?"

The two orderlies stood on the opposite side of the gurney where Gracie lay. They looked everywhere but at the doctor as he freed her from the straitjacket. Finally one of them said, "We thought we were doing the right thing, but maybe the right thing turned out to be the wrong thing."

"You think?!?!?"

"She was spouting off about an aunt living over in the office, Doc. Made no sense, see."

"Gracie, what are you talking about?"

Gracie looked back and forth from Dr. Knowles to the orderlies and grimaced.

"Gracie, please explain this. I know you can. Gracie?"

"Aunt Bernice Randall," whispered Gracie.

"Your aunt was a Randall, Gracie?"

"My father's oldest sister, Bernice Murray Randall."

"Gentlemen," Dr. Knowles said to the orderlies, "Gracie's aunt bequeathed the land and the buildings of about a quarter of this hospital campus. Please apologize to her and then get out of here."

"Doc, how would we have known that a patient would have a rich auntie like that? Ain't too likely now, is it?"

"I'm waiting, gentlemen."

"We in trouble here, Doc?"

"Not if you apologize quickly and make yourselves scarce."

"Sorry, sorry, Missy," mumbled both orderlies in tandem. They ran down the hall and left the doctor and Gracie alone.

"Gracie, what will I do with you?" Dr. Knowles said.

"Doctor, I've forgotten how to act outside of this ward, haven't I?"

"I'm afraid you have, my dear."

"What am I going to do?"

"You'll relearn, Gracie, my dear. You'll remember."

"Doctor, do you think I'm insane?"

"You just need help. We need to work on getting you well enough to get out of here. Rest today. We'll start again tomorrow. Okay?"

Gracie smiled, slid off the gurney, and made her way back to her bed. *You need to try harder,* she thought to herself. *Dammit all, you need to try harder to act sane. Tomorrow, you'll have to try harder. Yes, tomorrow!*

Chapter Nineteen

Gracie was definitely one of the more interesting patients Dr. Knowles had worked with in quite a while. She was bright, complicated, and had a family history that was puzzling. He decided he needed to find the time to read the letters that arrived shortly after she'd been admitted. He had simply stuffed them in her folder when they had arrived on his desk. Now he felt he needed to know more about this young woman. It took him a minute, but he found Gracie's folder in one of the stacks on his desk. The two letters were unopened. One had a return address from Mrs. William Glidden of Winslow, and the other was from Mrs. Wilfred Randall of Augusta. *Good grief,* thought Dr. Knowles. He tore open the latter.

It read:

> *To whom it may concern,*
> *My niece Grace Murray Grant is currently with you at the hospital. Please understand that she comes to you under very extenuating circumstances. She had a difficult childhood. Her father, my brother, was not a good provider. He drinks excessively. Three of his children were taken by the state when Gracie was a newborn. Her mother tried her best, but she was disabled and went to a sanitarium when Gracie and her younger brother were still quite young. The boy was taken by my sister and her husband, but Gracie was passed around among her mother's relatives. It is my understanding that she was not always treated well.*

> *This type of illness does not ordinarily run in the family. I feel there must have been problems in her marriage that added to Gracie's distress. Please do everything possible to help this young woman. Discretion with this information is requested, obviously. It is with utmost hesitancy that I write this to you.*
>
> *Sincerely,*
> *Mrs. Bernice Murray Randall*

Dr. Knowles remembered that he'd read Gracie's father had been a patient at the hospital in 1923 the year before she was even born. Knowles wondered if Mrs. Randall had written on behalf on her brother back then. He also wondered why she herself hadn't taken her niece in when her sister-in-law fell ill. He wondered if guilt had spurred the rich lady to write this letter now. Scanning down through Gracie's admittance papers again, his eyes fell on a notation that tugged at his heart. Gracie had arrived at the hospital with only a nightdress and a wedding band. Nothing else, and nothing had been brought to her. He closed her file. He'd read the other letter tomorrow.

Chapter Twenty

Gracie couldn't get out of her own head. These shock treatments didn't get any easier as time went on. How many had she actually had now? At three a week for how many weeks, she couldn't seem to remember. At least three, or was it four weeks? Maybe she would just float for the rest of today. Why wake up? She slowly became aware of someone sitting near her. Specifically on the foot of her gurney. Opening one eye slightly, she spied Cheryl Lee smiling at her. She smiled back with both eyes open. Gracie thought Cheryl Lee looked like how she imagined Tinker Bell in the story of Peter Pan. An ethereal little being.

"Gracie, you're awake!" Cheryl Lee tweaked Gracie's toes. "You were out for a long time after this treatment. Are you okay?"

"I'll survive, I guess. How 'bout you?"

"Oh, you know, the usual."

"What's the usual?"

"Well, since you asked, how did you get to do counseling with Dr. Knowles instead of Dr. Getchell? I don't want to work with Getchell anymore." Cheryl Lee smoothed her hospital top against her thighs over and over again. Gracie was familiar with this nervous tic of hers.

"Come sit closer to me." Gracie patted the space on the gurney next to her chest. "I can't see you well. These damned treatments blur my vision for a while." Gracie took a minute to see if any hospital personnel were around as Cheryl Lee scooted up closer.

"You're so lucky to be seeing Dr. Knowles," whispered Cheryl Lee.

"You've told me this, sweetheart, but then you refuse to tell me more. How can I understand if you won't tell me what you have against Getchell?"

Cheryl Lee gave Gracie a sideways glance and then murmured, "You don't have to talk to me like I'm a baby, Gracie. I think I might be older than you, so there. People don't think I have the sense to know what Getchell is doing to me, but I do, and it's not right."

"What does he do? Does he touch you in the wrong places?"

"Well, he just messes with me mostly, but a while back he took me to a private room, you know those few ones down the hall here, and told me to wait. In a few minutes he came back with an attendant and laughed about how he was giving him a going away present. That guy really hurt me, Gracie."

"Jesus, what did you do?" Gracie was now sitting up beside Cheryl Lee with her arms around her. Once again, they both looked up and down the hall.

"When the attendant left, I snuck out and down the hall to get back to the ward. I ran into Nurse Wight on my way. She helped me clean up and brought me back to my bed. She told me I'd been real bad and to never, ever tell anyone about it. I haven't 'til just now."

"Jesus H. Christ! We have to tell someone, Cheryl Lee. We have to. Getchell shouldn't be allowed to get away with that."

"Gracie, we can't. It happens. I've seen other women being taken out of the ward at night. Just help me get to talk to Dr. Knowles instead of Getchell. Maybe if you work with Knowles, Getchell won't bother you. Don't you think?"

"Good God, Cheryl Lee, this is a hell-hole, isn't it!" Gracie started to shiver. Cheryl Lee pulled her closer and rubbed her back.

"Gracie, don't get too upset. I didn't want to make you upset. I just..,"

"Ladies, what are you doing out here like this?" asked Nurse Downer as she approached the gurney they both sat on. "Gracie, didn't an attendant come to get you from your treatment? One should have by now. And just what are you doing here, Cheryl Lee? Really, sometimes both of you are such a bother. Cheryl Lee, jump down and come with me. Gracie, I'll call an attendant."

"Please don't!" snapped Gracie as she jumped down from the gurney. "I can walk with you two. I'm okay now." But she stumbled as she tried to move ahead with them.

Nurse Downer pushed her back onto the gurney. "I told you to wait here, please. Come along, Cheryl Lee. Now!"

The look on Cheryl Lee's face as she glanced back made Gracie nauseous. She closed her eyes tightly and told herself to just float and forget it. Float and forget it. In a few minutes, her gurney lurched and then started to move. Gracie feigned sleep. She couldn't open her eyes and look at the attendant, whomever he was. She just couldn't. She kept them closed through supper and into bedtime.

The next morning Gracie could not find Cheryl Lee anywhere in the ward. She did spy Nurse Downer and determined to approach her, but the nurse came to her before she had a chance to do it.

"We need to check your blood pressure, Gracie. Your dizziness was a little surprising. You usually don't have such weakness hours after a treatment. Let me see your left arm."

"This treatment seemed to really hit me hard, Nurse Downer, but I was also upset by something that Cheryl Lee told me. I'm wondering if I can share it with you in confidence, please."

"What could that little silly thing have told you that would upset you? Really now?"

"Can I tell you this without you telling everyone immediately, please?"

"Gracie Grant, now you have me just worried. Do please tell me what you are talking about."

"Well, it's about a doctor here in the hospital who did something very inappropriate to Cheryl Lee. It has upset me dreadfully."

"You aren't talking about her psychiatrist Dr. Getchell, are you Gracie?"

"Well, have you had suspicions, Nurse Downer?"

"Gracie, before you say anything you'll regret, let me explain something about Cheryl Lee to you. Her ability to understand the difference between truth and complete fiction is very limited. This wouldn't be the first time she has made up stories to get someone's attention and sympathy."

"What do you mean? She seems to be more aware of her surroundings than most of these patients, Nurse. You can't even carry on a conversation with over half of these poor things in here."

"She may be able to carry on a conversation, Gracie, but do you think that means she is telling the truth? Haven't you met a good liar before? There's a reason why Cheryl Lee has been here for years now. She's a compulsive liar with very little grasp of reality."

"But she seems so convincing. She really does. And I wouldn't trust Getchell as far as I could throw him."

Nurse Downer pulled her stethoscope out of her ears and glared at Gracie. The blood pressure cuff hugged Gracie's left arm as she looked at the nurse.

"Gracie, you need to be very careful about making trouble here. You're lucky that Dr. Knowles considers you bright and capable of recovery with therapy. Lots of these poor women are thought of as untreatable. Do you see them going out for sessions with either doctor? No, you don't. You don't want to rock the boat with something someone like Cheryl Lee is telling you. Don't you dare do that, now. I want to see you better and out of here. Be still for a minute now!"

Gracie watched the scowling nurse listen to the stethoscope in her ears. Then Nurse Downer yanked both the ends of the stethoscope out of her ears and pulled the cuff off Gracie's arm and announced, "Well, your blood pressure is sky high, Miss Gracie! Hope you're happy. Do yourself a favor: stay away from Cheryl Lee."

Gracie watched Downer stomp away. *Maybe it was a dream*, she thought to herself, but she remembered Dr. Getchell putting his hands somewhere that upset her when she'd first arrived. She'd been out of it, so the memory was hazy, but it was there. She also thought about the flirting she'd seen Nurse Downer do with Dr. Getchell. She sat pondering about whether or not to mention Cheryl Lee to Dr. Knowles at her next session. He seemed so nice, but her Aunt Violet had always told her never to trust anyone who wore pants, and unfortunately Dr. Knowles did.

Chapter Twenty-One

The fall air was downright cold that morning as the delivery men for the Harris Bakery on North Street in Waterville carried their trays off the loading dock and down to their trucks. Each truck waited behind the big bakery building with back doors open. Clouds of condensation from the heavy breathing of the workers could be seen in the brisk air as the labor was punctuated with the usual morning chatter.

One comment made Albert stop and whirl around with a tray of donuts tilting in his arms. Six packs of coconut-covered chocolates perched sideways on the edge of the tray as he barked, "What the Christ did you just say to me, Ovid?"

"Just speculating about that little missing wife of yours, Grantie." Albert's fellow bakery worker grinned at him. Ovid was a huge man with a round face. He had a reputation for not thinking before speaking. The men near him started to turn away, more aware of what was about to transpire than he was. Ovid continued, saying, "So, is it true she's in the nuthouse?"

Boxes of donuts flew as Albert tossed them, tray and all. He charged Ovid and sucker punched him. Ovid crashed in the driveway of the bakery. He howled and grabbed at his nose. Albert hovered over him.

"Get up and say that again, you stupid son of a bitch!" Albert stood with his fists squared off like a boxer as he leaned over him.

"Jesus, my nose!" whined Ovid. "Al, I was just joking. Come on!"

Phil Dunn was among the men Ovid had been talking with. Now he jumped in front of Albert and pushed him back.

"Do I have you to thank for this, Phil? Can't keep your friggin' mouth shut?" spewed Albert in Phil's face.

"It wasn't me, Al; everyone's been talking about it. Honest. Calm down. You don't want to hurt that stupid asshole really bad. We'll have to cover his route for him."

Two of their fellow bakery workers helped Ovid up. With his nose dripping blood, he babbled, "Good God, that little bastard has a punch. Who would of thought, huh? I think he broke my nose. I really do." His fellow workers walked him toward the office. Ovid stood a good head and shoulders taller than both of his helpers. At five foot six, Albert was shorter than all three of them. Phil was the only one Albert looked eye to eye with on the entire bakery delivery crew. He looked at the men walking away while Phil kept his hand on his shoulder. They both grinned when they overhead one man say to Ovid, "Christ, Ovid, didn't you know Grantie was a Golden Gloves for the state of Maine a few years back? Just flyweight, but he has a hell of a jab."

"Better figure out how you're gonna explain this to old man Harris, Al," said Phil.

"This is all I need, Phil. What the hell am I gonna do now?"

"Swallow your pride and get ready to beg to keep your job, I guess. What else can you do? You're gonna have to tell Harris what's really going on with little Gracie, so he'll maybe understand why you were so pissed. On top of that, even old Harris must realize what a friggin' mouthy idiot Ovid is."

"I hope you're right, Phil. I really do."

Later that day, after deliveries, Albert sat across a desk from his boss Mr. Harris. Fred Harris was a bespectacled man who looked like a Hallmark version of Santa. He rocked back in his office swivel chair and held his rotund middle as he gazed at his young employee. He waited.

"Listen, Mr. Harris, I don't know what got into me thinking I could attack Ovid that way. I'm really sorry, sir. Really I am," pleaded Albert.

Mr. Harris grinned. "Can you keep a secret, Grantie?"

Albert was surprised that his boss addressed him by his nickname. "Sure, sir."

"I've wanted to punch that fool for a while now. Thanks for doing it for me. He can't keep his orders straight to save his soul. My phone rings constantly with complaints, but I don't have the heart to let him go just now. He supports his two ailing parents, whom I know. They're good folk. Not their fault their son's not the sharpest knife in the drawer. "

"What?"

"Of course, now you must tell me why you did it, and we need to handle it somehow. You also need to tell me what's going on with you, son."

Albert walked out of Mr. Harris' office a half hour later not completely understanding what had just happened, but he was glad to have kept his job. He'd even apologize to poor Ovid and try to understand him more, as Mr. Harris had requested. It felt good to talk about his problems with a father figure like old Harris, even if he had embellished Gracie's diagnosis with the blood clot theory that was intended to give her illness a physical basis. Albert simply could not get his head around the information that doctor at Augusta State Hospital had told him about Gracie. It was too much! He decided to check on his little house in Winslow before going to Alley's. Maybe Stella would be around.

Chapter Twenty-Two

Gracie watched Dr. Knowles read through some papers at his desk. She sat with her legs pulled up and her arms wrapped around her knees. Finally, the doctor looked up at her.

"Gracie, your aunt writes to me about your troubled childhood. I think it would be helpful for us to talk about it in our sessions."

"I had a hard life, Dr. Knowles. Lots of people did where I came from. What good will hashing it over do? Grampa John told me not to whine and to look forward instead. I've tried to do that."

"Has that advice worked well for you, Gracie?" Dr. Knowles leaned forward in his chair.

Gracie put her feet on the floor. Her hand went up to the left side of her face as she looked away from the doctor. She started to rock in her chair.

"Gracie, maybe we can start by talking about that scar on your face again. You talked once before about comparing scars with a character by the name of Jackknife Fred. Your Aunt Bernice tells me your older three siblings were taken by the state. Do you remember that, Gracie?"

"Heavens, Doc, where do you want me to start? Let's see…I was a newborn when the town fathers came and snatched my sisters and brother. My mother told me she was lucky that they forgot to come back and get me once I was weaned. Such luck! I stayed with her and my drunken father for twelve more years and along came my little brother Ira John when I was eight. I've been a scarface since I was four and a German Shepard that belonged to a neighbor bit me after I fell into his pen. We didn't have money for a real doctor, so the neighbors fetched an old horse doctor to sew me up. Didn't do much of a job, did he? That about sums it up, now doesn't it, Doc?" Gracie laughed and then grimaced.

"Gracie, I thought the scar had something to do with your brother Ira John and goat's milk."

Gracie chuckled and said, "This scar had nothing to do with Ira John. Was my fault. I was too curious about a big dog."

Dr. Knowles looked at his patient. "Gracie, can you tell me what changed when you were twelve, please?"

Gracie peeked at the doctor. "That was a hard time for Ira John and me, Doc. Scary, you know."

"Why? Tell me about it, Gracie."

"It's hard to talk about." Gracie kept her hand covering her scar and sat without talking for a few minutes.

"Gracie, close your eyes and imagine being there as a twelve year old again. What was going on? Just tell me a story like you did when you introduced me to Jackknife Fred."

Gracie closed her eyes but didn't start talking.

"Gracie, where are you? Who do you see?"

"I don't see anyone. I'm alone. Running up the path behind our house to try to find Jackknife. Need his help. Bad. Kent had come home a few days back, and he was howling drunk. Went after Momma in that nasty way. Ira John and I hid behind the wood box, and I tried to cover his ears to keep him from hearing Momma cry. Nasty stuff hurts. The bastard got me and did that a couple times. God!" Gracie covered her face with her hands.

"Gracie, it's okay. You're safe now. Tell me; did you find Jackknife?"

"Had to bang and bang on his door. He opened it growling about how my old man owed him money. Then he noticed I was crying and asked me what was wrong. I told him that Momma had been sick in bed for days now after Kent roughed her up and left, and little Ira John and I had run out of food. I could cope with a noisy, empty stomach, but that little brother of mine was putting up an awful fuss. He was only four. Jackknife told me he had just made up a pot of baked beans, and he'd be glad to give me some to take back down home for the three of us. Told him I doubted I could get Momma to eat any, but Ira John and I would be obliged to him for beans."

Gracie's voice now sounded childlike. "Jackknife fixed two holes in a tin can and looped a piece of wire up as a handle, so I wouldn't burn my hands taking those hot beans home. He was so good to us." Gracie smiled for a minute with her eyes still closed. "But when I got back home, there was that big Packard in the front yard." She stopped talking again.

Dr. Knowles waited. Gracie was motionless. She loudly sucked up her breath.

"It was Aunt Bernice's car, you know. We were in for trouble when she bothered to drive to our shack on the outskirts of Windsor. And then I noticed Aunt Georgia was with her. Heard Aunt Bernice say to Georgia, 'Just hold your nose and come in with me.' Before I could head them off from knocking at the door, Ira John opened it up and greeted them. Georgia looked at him and gasped, 'Who is this little, filthy thing?' Aunt Bernice barked, 'Keep a civil tongue in your mouth, Georgie. This is your nephew Ira John. He can't be held accountable for our delinquent brother's behavior, now can he?' She turned to Ira John and asked him where our mother was. She never waited for an answer. Aunt Bernice pulled her sister in the door with her. They didn't notice me sneaking in behind them."

"Is this when the family was broken up again, Gracie?" Dr. Knowles kept a calm tone of voice.

"Yes. Aunt Bernice asked all the questions. Georgia just stood next to her with a handkerchief over her nose. 'Where's your mother? Why isn't she greeting us instead of this little boy? What on earth is that smell?' I told her Momma had been sick in bed, and I had to take care of Ira John and didn't keep up like I should with emptying Momma's thunder jug. Aunt Bernice pushed me aside and went into Momma's bedroom. She hollered for Georgia to come into the bedroom. I stood looking on at the two of them fussing over Momma. I had been busy with Ira John and hungry and hadn't looked in at Momma that particular day. They started talking about her being unconscious and all. I didn't know what to say. Just stood in the bedroom door and cried." Gracie was crying now as she continued talking to Dr. Knowles.

"Aunt Bernice said to me, 'Gracie, we are taking your mother to the hospital. She's bad.' Before I could say, 'I know,' she told me to get to bed with Ira John and wait for morning. Said she'd call my mother's brother William to come pick us up then. Georgia went on about how they should take us, too, but Bernice said they had their hands full with my mother. My mother's brother could help clean up some of the mess, too. She asked me if I'd seen my father. I told her no, and I didn't want to see him either. She laughed at that, I remember. They struggled getting Momma into the back seat of the Packard. Aunt Bernice repeated her instructions to me as I sat on Momma's footstool. I peeked over at Ira John. He was perched like a little chipmunk on the wood box. Bernice said, 'Gracie, can you manage being alone with your brother overnight?' I told her I'd been about alone with him for days. I was no baby. She asked about the can still in my hands and was glad to find out it was something to tide us over till tomorrow.

The car drove off, and Ira John jumped down off the wood box and jumped up and down like a puppy begging for something to eat. 'Aren't you worried about Momma?' I asked him. He said no, he was hungry, so we ate out of the can with our fingers. I did make him wash up before we climbed in bed. Ira John glued himself to me as we lay under the old quilt. Figured even though he was only four, he could feel the fear in the air just like me."

"Did your Uncle William arrive early the next morning for the two of you?" Dr. Knowles asked.

"No, but that's another long story, Doc. Seems everybody wanted a four-year-old boy, but nobody wanted me. I'm so tired. Please, can I go now?"

"Good enough for today, Gracie. Good enough."

Chapter Twenty-Three

Albert sat in his truck in the driveway of his Bassett Road house. This tiny structure seemed like a dollhouse compared to the big old farmhouse he had tried to save for his parents. Gracie had seemed so excited about having a house of her own without in-laws under foot, but soon she was complaining about the upkeep being too much for her. Too much? How long did it take to clean three small rooms? Granted, little Stevie's diapers had been hard to keep up with since they had limited water from the cistern on the roof, but really? Lots of women did with less, didn't they? Albert thought Gracie was used to hard work. He should have asked his mother to move in with them and help her even though the two of them didn't get along. Mother Ava had gone to live with his three sisters on a rotating basis and didn't seemed thrilled in any of those situations. Hard for her once his dad died, and they lost the farm in bankruptcy. He laughed out loud. *Right, that would have worked.* He could imagine Gracie fussing about that. *The two of them women in this miniature dwelling.*

Just then Stella walked out of her back door with a watering can. Stella, Stella, Stella. Albert remembered the last time he had been with Stella and how she let him hold her. Was she really attracted to him? Did she only pity him? What if Stella just wanted to break up the monotony of her married yet childless life on this forsaken side road in this tiny town where everyone knew everyone except for her? Stella was from "away." *It was partly her fault*, thought Albert. *Walking around on her lawn in the afternoon wearing lipstick and jewelry, then wondering why decent wives like Bunny Cates didn't know what to say to her.* But, oh, Stella was so nice to look at. Albert could hear his father rant, "Painted up potato of a woman. No better than a street walker. She's using you for a stud, Albert, my boy." That's what the old man would have said if he were still alive. But he wasn't.

Albert continued watching Stella watering her flowers on the side lawn of her house next to his Harris Bakery truck. He came here at the end of his work day to think about his life. Life, huh! His wife in Augusta State where he wasn't even allowed to visit her right now. Two baby sons being cared for by a dear old lady in Waterville who runs a laundry and a foster home.

His sister Ruth had chided him last Sunday after church about being a good Christian husband. What the hell did she know about his feelings as he watched Stella? Women never understood. His old man had died and left him with a farm in debt to his eyeballs. One of the reasons Gracie was so upset.

Stella put down her watering can and waved at Albert. He grinned back at her. He noticed her legs were shapely with narrow ankles like Gracie's. Not piano legs, straight up and down, like his mother's and sisters' legs. Albert considered himself a leg man. Never cared much for ample breasts. 'More than a handful is wasted,' his foster brother Bert would say at church camp as they hid in a grove of trees to sneak cigarettes. Albert grinned widely now.

Shit! Stella was walking toward his truck. She'd probably just want to flirt and hug him like she'd done before. Pity for the poor neglected neighbor with the sick wife.

"What are you grinning about, Al?" asked Stella when she stopped at the side door of the truck and placed her hands at the bottom of the window.

"Nothing, Stel," said Albert.

"Doesn't look like nothing." Stella rubbed his forearm that hung out the truck window.

"Silas around?"

"He's on a business trip. Company sent him to Portland for three days, Al." Now she leaned in close to Albert's grin.

"I need to get over to Waterville and check on my boys, Stel."

"Those baby boys can tell time, can they?"

"Well…"

"How about having a bit of supper? I made a roast up yesterday before I knew my husband was going to desert me. Shame to let it go to waste."

"Yes, it is."

Stella ran her hand over Albert's shoulder. He started to open the truck door. She stepped aside for the door and then let Albert pull her onto his lap. She nuzzled first one side of his face and then the other. Albert couldn't move. He was barely breathing.

"Al, would you like to come over to my house?"

"No time for that, Stel. There's no windows in the back of this bakery truck. Want to see where the donuts are stored?"

Stella grinned, turned around, and moved into the back with Albert following her. He helped her down on the truck floor like a gentleman, then leaned over her and started kissing her. Albert felt a sense of urgency and grabbed at the bottom of Stella's dress.

"Albert, this is a new dress. Give a lady a second. I'll slip it off." As she did that Albert pulled down his pants. He could do that without unbuckling them as he had lost so much weight recently.

Stella laughed and started to make a comment about his baggy pants when Albert was on top of her again. He yanked at her underwear and entered her quickly. It was over too soon, but Albert decided he needed to go for second helpings. Stella let him and enjoyed that time more. Albert collapsed next to her on the truck floor. They lay close to one another, smiling and looking up at the empty bakery racks that flanked them on both sides. Albert sat up suddenly.

"Stella?"

"I know, I know, Al…you need to go check on your boys." She placed her right index finger on his lips now.

"Can I take a rain check on the roast?" he babbled through her finger.

Pulling themselves together allowed for some self-conscious glances back and forth. As Stella stood back at the side door of his truck before

Albert drove off, she kissed him gently on his forearm. "Take care of yourself, Albert." She turned and walked away toward her house. Albert sat for a couple minutes watching her walk away. The pleasure of that sight seemed to overwhelm the slight sense of guilt that was creeping into him.

Chapter Twenty-Four

"What have you done, Al?" His sister Ruth scowled like no one else could. "Maybe you think you can fool Mollie and Mother, but they're gone now. You know you can't pull the wool over my eyes." She sat that Sunday afternoon with her baby brother at the back porch of the farm in Livermore that she ran with her husband and mother-in-law. Her husband Ernest was off in the barn with the cows. They watched Albert's sons Waynie and Stevie playing with her two girls and their beloved Tippy-dog.

"The boys miss Tippy."

"Don't change the subject. What brings you up here to sing in church and sit all nice with me?"

"I feel lost and so lonely, Ruthie. What am I supposed to do while Gracie is in that hospital?"

"You're to pray for strength and patience and look forward to the day you can visit your wife, Al."

"There are a lot of beautiful women out there, Sis. What harm would it do? Gracie wouldn't have to find out."

"Don't tell me any details. I just knew that's what it was."

"Why are you asking me about it then?"

Ruth stood up and straightened her apron. She waved at the children. "You aren't the only one who is not perfectly happy in their marriage, but a Christian follows what the good book says."

"The Bible doesn't have a book on what to do if your wife has a breakdown and is confined to a mental institution. They somehow didn't cover that."

"I have a meal to put on the table, Al." Ruth turned to go into the kitchen door.

Albert grabbed her hand. "Am I still invited, Sis?"

Ruth put her arm around Albert's shoulders and rested her cheek on the top of his head. "I'd do anything to have this not happen to you, Al. But it has, and you can't just let go of your commitment to Grace. You can't."

"You're right, Sis." Ruth and Albert's moment was interrupted by the squawking of one of the kids. "You get dinner ready. I'll deal with these characters," Albert offered.

Dinner in Ruth's dining room was a lively affair. Four children under five years of age provided entertainment. Ruth flew around the table and in and out of the kitchen too much to eat the meal on her own plate. Her burly husband, naked from the waist up, sat and ate at one head of the table. Totally oblivious to her son's dinner table decorum or lack of it, Ernest's mother was at the other end. Both seemed to ignore any goings-on until Ernest turned to Albert and asked, "Where the hell is Gracie?"

"Ernest, I've explained the situation to you," said Ruth, stopping briefly at his elbow on one of her trips to the kitchen.

"I don't remember, Ruthie. Thought I'd ask. What's happening to her, Al?"

Albert dropped his fork in his plate. He noticed all the children had quieted except for baby Stevie who was busily making a mushy mess of his potatoes and peas on his plate. "Gracie is not well, Ernest."

"I should say she isn't. Haven't seen her for a while now."

"Ernest, we can discuss this when little ears are not around," said Ruth, returning from the kitchen with a pie in her hands. "Who's ready for dessert?"

Albert looked across the table at his two-and-a-half-year-old son Waynie who was looking at him with soulful eyes. His niece Linda poked Waynie and made him squeal and jab her back. Everyone dug into blueberry pie, and Gracie was forgotten.

Later that afternoon as all four children, Ruth's bare-chested husband, and her mother-in-law napped, Ruth sat with Albert at the back porch again. She had her eyes closed, but her lips were moving.

"You're praying for me, aren't you, Sis?" Albert reached for his sister's hand.

"Someone has to pray for your sweet soul, Al. I love you dearly, so it might as well be me."

"Do you consider me a sinner?"

"No, my dearest, I consider you a man of God. A man who will find his way and do the right thing by his wife and children."

"But you're still praying for me." Albert grinned at Ruth.

Ruth blew her brother a kiss. "Won't hurt, now will it?"

Chapter Twenty-Five

October 26th. I think it's October 26th. My 24th birthday, and here I am in this hellhole. Gracie stood in the ward at the window closest to her bed and tried to peer out through the heavy wire inserts.

"Are you talking to yourself again, Gracie?" asked Miss Downer as she approached the window.

"Lord, you know how to startle someone!" Gracie hugged herself with her arms and turned to look at Miss Downer. "I was just wondering if today was the 26th."

"All day long, Gracie. What's special about today? Wait, is it finally your birthday?"

Gracie turned away and looked out the window again. Miss Downer grabbed Gracie's hands in hers and turned her around. "Gracie, happy birthday! Can you think of happier times when you had a party or something?"

"No one ever celebrated any birthday of mine," said Gracie. "Never was any money to party with anywhere I was, that's for sure."

"Maybe your next birthday will be a great one with a decorated cake and presents. You just need to worry about getting well, Gracie. By the way, Dr. Knowles would like to see you for a session in a few minutes."

"Good, I'd like to talk to him, too." Grace said a bit louder.

"Gracie, do you remember our conversation recently?"

"The one about not running my mouth off about other people's problems?"

"Gracie, you're wrong about Cheryl Lee and Dr. Getchell. I'm sure you are."

"When I was first here, dear Dr. Getchell put his hand on one of my breasts when he was supposedly examining me. I was a bit hazy with drugs, but I do remember it, Nurse Downer."

Miss Downer stiffened her posture and replied, "Grace, how could you remember something that happened when you were first here. Do you remember how out of it you were? Dr. Getchell would not have done something like that to you in the condition you were in. He's not like that."

Gracie and Miss Downer stood glaring at one another. Gracie then slouched against the window sill and hung her head. Miss Downer put her hands on Gracie's shoulders.

"Gracie, you are getting better. Dr. Knowles is encouraged by the results of your treatments and his sessions with you. Please don't blow everything by going in and telling him your theory about Cheryl Lee. He gave up on her years ago. I'm surprised Dr. Getchell even still tries to help her once in a while."

"Right, he tries to help her."

"Gracie, part of your diagnosis involved paranoia. If you start telling stories about Cheryl Lee, Dr. Knowles will think you're regressing. Lord only knows what he'll decide to do then."

Gracie said nothing at first. She looked into Miss Downer's eyes. They seemed to show sincerity. "Okay, okay, I won't say anything to him today, but will you please promise me this? Would you keep an eye on Cheryl Lee? She seemed to be telling the truth to me. Why would she lie to me?"

"For attention, Gracie, since she is really just a child regardless of her actual age, but I'll keep an extra watch on her. Off to see Dr. Knowles now."

Gracie walked along the halls of the hospital on her way to Dr. Knowles' office and thought about the drabness of the pea green color on the walls. Then going through the tunnel that connected the patient wards to the back building where the offices were always unnerved her. Always afraid she might run into a creepy orderly, she quickened her pace and soon arrived at the doctor's door. She knocked and held her head to his door to listen.

"Knock like you mean it, Gracie!" shouted Dr. Knowles.

Gracie giggled and rapped harder at the door.

"Who's there?"

"Dr. Knowles, you know it's me." Gracie rested her head against his door once more. *I like this character even if he is a man.* "May I come in?" Gracie asked.

"By all means, young lady. Do enter my humble office. Such as it is."

Gracie opened the door and stepped into the office. She was grinning ear to ear.

"I got you to smile, now didn't I, Miss Gracie. How are you today?"

"It's my twenty-fourth birthday, Doc."

Dr. Knowles smiled at Gracie. "Move those file folders and sit down with this old man then."

When Gracie had settled, she looked at Dr. Knowles with her usual sober expression. "What do you want me to talk about today, Doc?"

"Gracie, the last time we talked you mentioned your father doing "nasty things" to your mother. You also added that he had done those to you. Can you talk any more about that?"

Gracie looked at her lap. "I don't remember saying that."

"It would help you to talk a little about it if you can, Gracie."

"I could tell you about my mother's fancy glass Sears Roebuck washboard. That's quite the story, Doc."

"Start any way you would like to, Gracie." Dr. Knowles had his wire-rimmed glasses off and was chewing on the end of one bow as he looked expectantly at Gracie.

"Well, Ira John, Mom, and I had just come home from selling soap. Think I was about eleven, so my brother was three or so. My mother had discovered the Celestial Soap Company because they ran an ad on the radio. The idea was you could keep a bit of money from every bar you sold. There wasn't much my mother could do to earn money with her lameness, so this seemed the answer to our problems. She sent away for her first sales kit as soon as she had saved the money out of what little funds Kent would give her from time to time. When we went out, I would help with carrying the goods, and Ira John would be the cute thing who might get us in people's doors. This day we had sold quite a bit, and Mom was excited and tired out, too. She plunked down in her rocking chair and fell asleep.

Ira John curled up on the wood box with our old dog. I decided to sneak a nap on my parents' bed. It was a mistake."

Gracie was quiet for a couple minutes.

"It's okay. You're safe with me, Gracie," Dr. Knowles said.

Gracie sat upright and continued. "Woke up to a horrible crash and then Kent hollering at my mother. I sat up on the bed and was wondering if Ira John was able to hide when Kent came into the bedroom. He says, 'Look at the little princess who's taken over her father's bed.' I hollered for my mother, but she didn't answer. Kent sat on the edge of the bed and says, 'Let Daddy just nap with you, little girl,' and he grabs at me. I tried to get away from him, but he had a firm grip on me with one hand and was groping my chest with the other one. 'Aren't you ever gonna grow anything up there, Gracie girl?' he says. And that's when I remembered what Aunt Vi said to do to him when he got this way. I pulled my leg around and kicked him hard right where it counts. Lord, did he holler!"

Gracie let out a weak laugh and then said, "Soon's he straightened up, he was after me. I had made it to the kitchen, but he was right behind me. Son of a bitch wasn't as drunk as I thought he was, see? Momma was on the floor by her rocker. Ira John was nowhere in sight. I spied my mother's new glass washboard leaned up against the washtub. Was a stool by it 'cause I would stand there and help Momma with the wash. I jumped up on that stool and grabbed that washboard. Kent was next to me by then. I held the washboard high over my head. Kent looked at me with a leering grin and reached for me. I brought that washboard down on his head as hard as I could. That stopped him. He was motionless on the floor not far from Momma. I didn't care if Kent was dead or alive, but I was scared about Momma."

Gracie held her face in her hands. Dr. Knowles wanted to let her cry for a few minutes, and he was startled when suddenly she looked up and continued.

"I was in a daze, I guess, when I heard Jackknife Fred holler, 'What the hell is going on here, child?' I looked and there was Ira John behind him. He must have run up to his shack to get him. Smart little fellow, that Ira John. Kent started to stir on the floor. I told Jackknife that Kent was after me. He looked mean when I told him that. Didn't know if he was mad at me or what. 'Take Ira John outside, Gracie. Now!' I did just that. We waited outside the door. Listened but didn't dare look in. Jackknife said some mean things to Kent. Scared me. Hoped Ira John didn't understand all of what was said but I wasn't sure. Jackknife came out and found us. He picked up Ira John and carried him on his hip and told me to follow. I asked where we were going, and he said home with him for a while. 'What about Momma?' I asked. Jackknife said Kent wouldn't be bothering my mother tonight."

"Did you go back home soon?" asked Dr. Knowles.

"Next day. Kent was gone. Momma was limping a bit more than usual, but she was up and moving. She said a brisk thank you to Jackknife, and he left. When he was gone, she started scolding me about her shattered washboard. Said things like 'Why couldn't you hit your father with a stick of wood?'"

"Wasn't she worried about you?"

"Nope, no one ever was worried about me, Doc, except for Aunt Vi, and then she told me never to tell anyone when Kent messed with me because it would bring shame to the family. One time she cleaned me up and said 'Thank God, you're not able to pay dearly for this yet.' I didn't know what she meant at the time. Now I do."

"That's as much sympathy as she gave you?"

"Yep, told me all men are bastards. Don't ever trust one of them."

"Gracie, I hope you discovered that isn't always true."

"I don't know. I'm really tired, Doc."

Gracie sat quietly for a few minutes. Dr. Knowles suggested she go back to the ward to rest.

Chapter Twenty-Six

After supper that warm October evening Albert told Mrs. Alley he needed to get something at his Bassett Road house. He wanted to take the boys. He babbled to Alley about the boys needing to see their own house. He wasn't very convincing, he'd guessed, as Alley gave him a puzzled look and told him fine.

"If Stevie is overtired, you're dealing with putting him to bed, not me," Alley told him as he was leaving.

Carrying Steve on his right hip, Albert went out the door to his bakery truck with Wayne in tow. He placed them both in the passenger side. Wayne held his squirmy little brother as Albert started the truck. They drove along with the windows halfway down.

"You excited about seeing our house again?" Albert asked Wayne.

"Where's Momma?" asked Wayne.

Albert glanced at his older son. At slightly more than two-and-a-half years old, Wayne startled Albert with his desire to understand what was going on. He also thought him an articulate little bugger.

"Do you remember we talked about Momma being away for a while because she was sick? Remember that, Punkie?"

"Where is she being sick?"

"Well, she's in a hospital far away. She's getting better the doctor says."

"Wanna see her."

"Mom, Mom, Mom!" chanted fourteen-month-old Steve.

"We wanna see Momma!" said Wayne a little louder.

They both started chanting "Momma" louder and louder.

"Stop that, both of you!" yelled Albert. They stopped. Steve started quietly crying as Wayne hugged him tightly. Albert stared out at the road and drove the three miles to Bassett Road too fast. He pulled in the yard just as Steve had fussed himself to sleep. Wayne still glared at him as he stopped the truck.

"Ready to go in with me?" he asked Wayne.

"Baby's asleep."

"I'll take Stevie." He cradled the sleeping Steve with his right arm and hoisted Wayne on his left hip. He juggled the boys as he opened the back door of the tiny house. The kitchen seemed chilly with the oil stove off. Life in this little place with his family seemed a distant dream to Albert. Wayne wriggled down his leg and to the floor. He ran into the bedroom off the kitchen.

"Momma? Momma?" Wayne's voice stabbed at Albert.

"Waynie, Momma's not here. She's in that hospital I told you about," Albert said as he walked into the bedroom to retrieve his son.

"I wanna see Momma," half-sobbed Wayne.

"So do I, kid. So do I," said Albert.

"Where is she, Daddy?" Albert was kneeling in front of Wayne now. Steve snuggled into his neck and didn't seem to wake even with all the movement and talking.

"I shouldn't of brought you here, Punkie," whispered Albert to Wayne, grabbing his left hand. Wayne pulled away from his father and stamped his feet on the wood floor.

"I want Momma! Now!" Albert admired the peanut's passion. He just wished he could somehow explain what had happened to his mother in a way that he would understand.

"Let's go, son," said Albert as he reached out for his hand again. This time Wayne took his father's hand and let him lead the way out to the kitchen. "Do you remember playing here, Punkie? Remember wrestling with Tippy?"

"No," said Wayne, not looking up at his father. "Want Alley!"

"Okay, we'll go back."

As Albert was closing the back door, he heard Wayne say hi to someone. His heart pounded in his chest a couple times. *Of course she saw the truck.* He looked up and smiled at Stella. She was petting Wayne's blonde head.

"You brought your entourage tonight," said Stella.

"Yes, I thought they might enjoy seeing their old house, but it didn't seem to help," said Albert.

"Momma's far, far way," said Wayne to Stella.

"I know," said Stella, looking at Albert instead of Wayne. Albert looked away.

"Alley loves us now," explained Wayne to Stella.

"I'm glad she does. You be a good boy now. Bye!" Stella turned and walked back toward her house.

"Stella, wait…" said Albert.

"Not now, Al. Not now." She walked across the side lawns. Albert stood watching her until Wayne tugged at his pant leg.

"Want Alley, Daddy."

His father didn't answer him. When Stella had closed her door, he grabbed Wayne up and walked to the truck. He drove the three miles back to Boutelle Avenue slowly. When he arrived, both boys were sound asleep, nestled against him. He sat in his truck for a long time. Something dripped on the front of his shirt right where Harris Bakery was embroidered. He made himself grin when he pondered if it was tears or snot. *Good God!*

Chapter Twenty-Seven

Everything was quiet in Ward 5 except for Ester's incessant mumbling coming from the middle part of the room. Gracie had become so used to that sound she hardly noticed it at all. The middle of the afternoon was when patients' medications would kick in, and many napped. Gracie liked this time of day. She could ignore the cots to the right of hers. Her cot was tucked up to the farthest left corner of the ward, almost by itself. She pretended she was alone. She had never had a chance to be all alone. Her whole life had been spent taking care of others. She never had an opportunity to think just of herself and what she needed. Dr. Knowles asked her what she wanted for herself. She replied with a facetious comment intended to take the pressure off the session and the attention away from herself as she had always done with people. The question scared her. She'd thought a husband and children were what she wanted since she had no chance of going on to school after high school graduation. She didn't want to stay at Mrs. Alley's laundry, running a hot mangle and helping with all those foster kids. It was like she'd never gotten away from her uncle's farm where she was nothing but a glorified maid and babysitter.

If she was as smart as her teachers had told her she was, why didn't she realize that married life would be a continuation of what she had always done? *The first female recipient of the Bausch and Lomb Science Award in the history of Winslow High School changing diapers for two baby boys while hauling water and nursing the younger one. She got so tired, so damned tired.* Why did the whole scene seem like a blur to her now? Had her sister Flippie visited and scolded her about looking so poorly? She couldn't remember.

Damned Flippie! Always so bossy the few times she got to be older sister. Almost as bad as her oldest sister Cora. At least Cora lived too far away to visit very often. But Ira John; what was that little tyke doing right now? Running their Aunt Edie ragged, probably. He would be almost sixteen years old soon. *No one worried about me when I was that age. Don't know why I'm worried about that little fart.* Gracie felt a gnawing pain in her stomach. She chuckled to herself and wondered if it was despair or just hunger. It was a while before supper was to be served. *Jesus, Grace Murray Grant, how will you get yourself out of this situation?*

"Gracie?"

"Miss Downer," Gracie replied.

"Dr. Knowles wants to know if you would like to see your Uncle Bill and Aunt Lucy." the nurse said as she sat on the foot of Gracie's cot.

"What? Are they here?"

"Not right now, but they have asked about coming to see you. They told the doctor you lived with them for several years. It might be good to see them, Gracie. What should I tell the doctor?"

Gracie looked at the nurse and said nothing. *Smarten up and act appropriately,* Gracie's inner self told her. "Okay, when will they visit?"

"Soon, Gracie. I'll tell the doctor." Nurse Downer jumped up and ran off.

"Shit!" said Gracie out loud. Ester stopped mumbling for a few seconds. Gracie said no more and the mumbling resumed.

Soon turned out to be very soon. Gracie was told to get ready for a visit the next day.

"Gracie, shall I help you with your hair?" asked Cheryl Lee.

"Why?" Gracie almost snarled at her.

"Don't you want to look pretty for your relatives?"

"Spent most of my time when I lived with them on my hands and knees scrubbing their kitchen floor," said Gracie. Then she softened when she saw Cheryl Lee's disappointment. "Shit on a shirt, go ahead. See if you can do anything with this thin mop."

Having her hair brushed soothed Gracie. She closed her eyes for a few minutes and tried to tell herself to behave and be good when Uncle Polly and Aunt Lucy were with her. *People are funny and not always "ha ha" funny Mom used to say. Maybe they feel a little guilty?*

"Shall you look in a mirror, Gracie?" asked Miss Downer when she joined the two women.

"No thanks, I'll trust Cheryl Lee. What I imagine will be better than what I'd actually see, Nurse," said Gracie. She stood up and straightened her hospital garb. "Do you think it would be all right if I asked them to bring me a dress?"

"Don't see why not. Let's go to the visitors' lounge." Gracie allowed the nurse to lead her by the hand to see her relatives.

Aunt Lucy sat on a sofa and grinned as Gracie entered the lounge. Gracie understood her not getting up to greet her. It took Lucy some time to get up off a piece of furniture at her size. Gracie just hoped the cheap furniture in this place would hold her. She looked around the room for her uncle. She spied him pacing back and forth at the further end of the room.

"William, William, she's here!" said Lucy from her perch. "Get over here, for God's sake. Hi, dear!"

Gracie stood in front of her aunt still holding the nurse's hand. Nurse Downer pulled her hand away and said, "I'll give you a minute, Gracie. Everything okay?"

Gracie said nothing. She looked at the nurse who hadn't moved away from her yet.

"Good God, isn't she talking yet? We assumed she'd be talking again after all this time in this place," said Lucy to the nurse.

"She's fine," the nurse replied to Lucy. "Aren't you, Gracie? Say hello to your aunt."

"Gracie, dear, good to see you," said her uncle as he wrapped an arm around her shoulders before she had a chance to say anything.

"Hi, Uncle Polly." Gracie smiled at him.

"Uncle Polly? Where's Bill?" asked the nurse.

"It's what we always called him even though his name is Bill, or really William," said Gracie.

"Come sit with us, Gracie," said Polly, leading his niece to a couch near the one his wife dominated. "You look pretty good, dear."

Gracie looked around and noticed they were the only ones in the lounge. Nurse Downer had quietly disappeared. She sat with her uncle and looked first at him and then at Lucy.

"Thanks for fibbing well, Uncle Polly. I'm afraid I'm a mess."

"Sweetheart, don't they allow you to at least have decent clothes?" asked Lucy.

"Lucy, please. She looks fine now," said Polly.

Gracie laughed. "You're right, Aunt Lucy. These hospital things are ridiculous. Can't tell if it's meant to be a dress for the day or a gown for night. Maybe that's the point. To keep us in limbo and quiet."

Polly and Lucy both looked at her and waited. Gracie wrung her hands in her lap until her uncle reached over and grabbed them.

"Is there anything we can do to help, Gracie?" he asked.

"Short of getting me out of this hellhole, it would be nice if you could get a decent outfit to me somehow."

"I don't know how many times we can get down here, Gracie," said Lucy.

"Now, Lucy, hush. We'll get something to you, dear. Least we can do is get after Albert to pack a bag and bring it down. I assume he's visiting you?" Polly looked at his niece.

"Isn't he?" asked Lucy too.

Gracie tipped her head down and started rocking slightly. Her aunt and uncle watched.

"Polly, go call for the nurse," said Lucy.

"No, please, I'm okay," said Gracie. "I'm just so tired. I'm still really so tired."

"Of course, Gracie. You need to rest as much as possible, so you can get home to your family soon," said Polly.

"I will. I'll be good; I promise. I'll take care of the boys and the house. You'll see. I promise," repeated Gracie.

"We know, Gracie. Now your uncle and I have to go soon as we have a church meeting to get to today, I'm afraid," said Lucy.

"What?" asked Uncle Polly.

"You old fool, you don't remember anything I tell you. The one I mentioned yesterday, Polly Glidden. About the visiting missionaries." Lucy started struggling to get off the couch.

Polly jumped up and helped her.

"If we had a meeting, we shouldn't have driven all the way down here, Lucy," he said as he tugged on both of his wife's arms. They both stood in front of Gracie now. She stood up, too.

"Thank you for coming down," said Gracie as she looked at the floor.

"You take care, Gracie," said Lucy, and she patted Gracie's shoulder.

Polly hugged his niece, but she remained limp in his arms. Lucy turned and started walking out. Polly stood for a few minutes with his hands still on Gracie's shoulders.

"Life has not been fair to you, my Gracie," said Polly. "Try to come back to us if you can. We all miss you. Shirley asks about you every day. Pray to the heavenly father for support, dear. I pray for you, too."

"Polly, come on!" Gracie and Polly looked at the door of the lounge to see an impatient Lucy waiting.

"Go ahead, Uncle Polly. This place must be horrible to visit."

"No, Gracie. Your Aunt Lucy just doesn't understand some things. We'll get some clothes to you, dear."

Gracie nodded her head and her uncle left to catch up with his wife. Gracie plunked back down on the couch. That was where Nurse Downer found her a few minutes later.

"Heavens! That was a short visit. Well, I hope it was good to see them, Gracie," said the nurse before she saw Gracie's face.

"A real chuckle, Nurse Downer," said Gracie through tears.

"Gracie, don't cry now. It's always hard to see family again at first. Things will get easier; you'll see. Let's get you back to the ward for some rest."

"I guess that's where I belong now, isn't it?" She walked obediently with the nurse out of the lounge.

Chapter Twenty-Eight

Dr. Knowles watched Gracie from across his desk. Her body language upset him. She had regressed after the short visit from the outside world. After a series of twenty-one shock treatments and some successful sessions with him, he thought she would do better with her visit from her aunt and uncle. The shy fetal position with her arms wrapped around her legs that were pulled up underneath her and her head on her knees was presenting to him this morning. He got no smile from her with his 'knock on the door like you mean it' joke. He continued to keep his eye on her as he pretended to be rearranging files on his desk. She suddenly looked up from her knees and scowled at him.

"Okay, Gracie, tell me what you're thinking."

"It's not pretty, Doc."

"Then let's air it out, Gracie. Might make you feel better."

Gracie stamped her feet down onto the office floor. She rearranged her clothing for a minute and then looked at the doctor.

"Why the hell would they want to come see me here when they never wanted me in their home in the first place?" said Gracie.

"Your aunt and uncle? They told the hospital you were like a daughter to them."

"Daughter, my ass!" Gracie blurted, then, "Sorry, Doc."

"Gracie, I'd rather see you angry than withdrawn. Why do you feel they never wanted you?"

"Because they never did. They only agreed to take me so they could have my little brother Ira John. It was supposed to be a package deal; they already had three little girls of their own and wanted a boy. When they found out my father's side took Ira John, they didn't want me. My other uncle, Polly's younger brother Cliff and his wife were shamed into coming to get me. My grandfather John told everyone it would make the family look bad if one side took one of us and nobody took me. Uncle Cliff and his wife Doris didn't want a half-grown girl any more than they wanted a stray cat."

Gracie bit her lip and looked out the window.

"Gracie, remind me how old you were when your mother was sent to the sanatorium, please."

"Twelve. A skinny, scar-faced twelve-year-old with a foul mouth, according to my Uncle Cliff's wife Doris. She was something else, that one. Made me wear dog-turd curls in my hair the first day of school while I was staying with them."

Dr. Knowles grinned. "What on earth are dog-turd curls, Gracie?"

"You people from out of state don't know anything, do you, Doc?"

"How do you know I'm from out of state?"

"That's what the nurses and attendants say when they're fussing about you, Doc."

"Really. Okay, what's a dog-turd curl?"

"When you curl your hair with rags but don't comb out the curls after you remove the rags. Looks like old dog turds. The joke was on her because I made a friend on the bus who combed them out for me before we got to school. Ethel Hapworth. I really was obliged to her for helping me."

"Then how did you end up with your Uncle…Polly, do you call him?"

"Easy, Doc. Wasn't long before handsome Uncle Cliff took too much of a liking to me. Doris never noticed, but Grandpa John did at a Christmas gathering. Overheard him scolding Cliff and telling him to pack me up and bring me to the farm. That was Grandpa John's farm, where Polly and his family lived with him."

"Did he actually take advantage of you, Gracie?"

"No, he didn't. Don't know if he would have, to tell you the truth. He was young and foolish. Think he might have been trying to piss off his wife by flirting with the likes of me. Anyway, I became the maid and nanny at the farm. Polly and Lucy already had the three girls, and Patsy was born shortly after I arrived. I worked my ass off while I was there."

"How did they treat you otherwise?"

"Like hired help, Doc. I broke my ankle playing basketball in gym when I started high school. Told me I'd heal on my own and never took me to see a doctor. Damned ankle still aches on a damp day."

"I'm sorry, Gracie. Did anything inappropriate happen to you there?"

"Yes, I was forced to attend the Advent Christian Church. What a bunch of pompous jerks went to that church! And of course, that's where I met Albert and the whole Grant family."

"I see. That's how you met your husband. He didn't attend the same school?"

"Oh, no, he was a Lawrence Bulldog. Graduated early since he was so smart. Then he stayed home to work on his father's farm."

Gracie looked down at her lap.

"You waiting for me to start spieling about Albert now?" she asked.

"Do you want to?" Dr. Knowles leaned as far forward as he could on his desk and studied Gracie's face.

"I told Cheryl Lee I'd come read with her this afternoon. You know her?"

"Of course, Gracie. Go ahead."

Chapter Twenty-Nine

Gracie was delighted with her job in the hospital library. Miss Downer had helped her get it, and it was certainly better than working in the laundry where many of her ward-mates labored. That little nurse drove her nuts sometimes, but she did seem to genuinely care. The hospital library was really just one big room. Couldn't have been more than three or four thousand books, Gracie figured. Nothing like her beautiful Lithgow Library in Winslow. Gracie giggled out loud when she thought about how she had told Aunt Lucy she had to go do research at that library after school to avoid doing the damned housework Lucy had lined up for her. Uncle Polly would pick her up after his shift at the Hollingsworth and Whitney Paper Mill. He admired his niece's brains, he would always tell her. Used to tell her that her housework would be still be there when she got home. Unfortunately he was right.

Mrs. Philbrook, the librarian of the one-room library, sat quietly at her desk by the door as Gracie passed the duster over the tops of the books. Gracie peeked over at her. She figured Mrs. Philbrook had to be in her eighties. She looked older than Old Lady Stimson who lived down from the farm in Winslow, and she was seventy-five. Plus, she hadn't moved since she sat down after giving Gracie the duster. Maybe she was asleep behind those thick glasses. Gracie took a break from dusting and pulled out a book. *Of Mice and Men. Funny title.* Gracie remembered wading through Mr. Steinbeck's *Grapes of Wrath* in her senior English class. Had oddly made her feel good to realize that some people had it worse than she did in life. This one looked shorter and easier than *Grapes of Wrath*. Maybe she would ask Mrs. Philbrook if she could borrow it. It didn't look like it had had much use.

"Gracie, Gracie," Gracie suddenly heard, and she looked up from the book she had just opened.

"Cheryl Lee? What are you doing here?"

"I'm on my way from the laundry room and was able to sneak by a snoozing Mrs. Philbrook," said Cheryl Lee. "What a cozy job you have here, Gracie!"

"You won't get in trouble sneaking in here instead of returning to the ward?"

"Well, never mind, Gracie. Guess you want this place all to yourself," said Cheryl Lee. She looked down at the floor.

"I don't mean it that way, Cheryl Lee. I just don't want you to give that old battle-ax of a Nurse Wight any reason to be angry with you," Gracie said.

"Nurse Wight was born angry. Nothing we do can change that, Gracie."

"You're right, but please lower your voice. This is a library." Gracie showed her friend the Steinbeck book she had in her hands.

Cheryl looked at the book and asked, "Will you read it to me? I don't read so well."

"I have to ask to borrow it, but I will if it is okay with Mrs. Philbrook."

"Yes!" squealed Cheryl Lee. She hugged Gracie.

Gracie pulled her friend away from her and started to shush her when they heard Mrs. Philbrook.

"What is going on here? Gracie, who is this patient?" asked the librarian.

"Gracie told me I could visit her, didn't you, Gracie?" said Cheryl Lee.

"Well, I really don't remember saying that," said Gracie.

"I should have known better than to trust that young nurse. Grace, you put that book back, and you and your friend get back to the ward," said Mrs. Philbrook.

"We don't want your old books anyway," said Cheryl Lee as she passed by the librarian.

Gracie put the book back on the shelf and paused in front of Mrs. Philbrook.

"I'm sorry, but you don't understand, Mrs. Philbrook," Gracie began.

"Do I need to call an orderly?"

"No, ma'am."

Gracie left the library and looked for Cheryl Lee in the hall. She saw her running way ahead of her. Cheryl Lee's arms were up at her sides, flapping as if she were a bird. Gracie walked slowly back to Ward 5.

Later that day, Nurse Downer found Gracie sitting meditatively on the edge of her bed. She sat down beside her.

"What were you thinking? Allowing Cheryl Lee to help you in the library?" Nurse Downer asked her.

"She just showed up, and I didn't have the heart to shoo her away. I never thought she would be rude to Mrs. Philbrook like that."

"Maybe now you see what I mean about your friend being like a child," said the nurse.

Gracie just looked at Nurse Downer.

"Well, Gracie, do you know how to fold laundry, my dear?" asked the nurse.

"Unfortunately, I do," replied Gracie. "All too well, I know. On top of that, my hair all long and straggly like this makes me look like a wash woman, doesn't it?"

Miss Downer looked Gracie over and smiled. "We need to do something about your hair. It's a great sign that you're worried about it. You're coming back to us, Gracie."

"I guess so. What other choice do I have?"

"How about letting me cut your hair? I can do it just like mine. Do you like my hairstyle?" Miss Downer was passing her hands through Gracie's locks.

"Mine will never look as good as yours. It's much thinner."

"You're a pretty young woman, Gracie. Please just let me try."

"I guess so. Maybe you can do something with this hair, but you can't fix this scarred face, now can you, Miss Downer?" Gracie put her left hand over her face.

"Don't be silly, Gracie. That scar barely shows. I need to sign out. I'll come back and get you. We can set up our beauty shop in Mrs. Wight's office. We'll clean up very carefully, so she'll never find out a thing. See you soon." Miss Downer turned and almost danced out of the ward. Gracie suddenly felt self-conscious as she noticed a few other patients looking her way.

Chapter Thirty

No sign of her, thought Albert that afternoon as he sat in his bakery truck looking at Stella's house. He pushed open the truck door and walked over to his mailbox. He wasn't expecting any mail, but this angle gave him a better look at Stella's front windows. He was startled to feel an envelope as he reached into the box while straining to see into his neighbor's living room window. He pulled the piece of mail out and glanced at the return address. It was a familiar handwriting. Albert felt scolded before he even considered opening the letter and reading its contents. His sister Ruth must have spoken to her, and now here was his comeuppance.

Albert sat on the half-open back of the bakery truck, ripped open the envelope and looked at the letter. Written in a teacher's perfect penmanship, his mother wrote:

> My dearest son,
>
> The Lord has given you a true test at a very young age. I know you are up to dealing with this. Your sisters and I are praying for you every day. You know what your father would have instructed you to do in this trying time. Keep your commitment to your marriage and your family, Albert. Please bring the boys down to see me when you can. I miss them. I wish I was

strong enough to care for them, my dear. The Lord is testing me with this illness at a bad time and keeping me from helping my loved ones as I would like to be able to do. Take care and keep faith, my boy.

Much love,
Mother

Damn that Ruth! Wait 'til I see her this weekend. Albert jumped back in his truck and took off to Waterville to see his boys. He was still fussing about his sister when he was greeted by Mrs. Alley near the front door of the boarding house.

"Al, those relatives from over on Cushman Road called and said Gracie would like to have some of her own clothes at the hospital. Isn't that great?" said Mrs. Alley.

"What's so great about it, Alley?"

"For the love of God, Al, sometimes you men are so thick! It means she's feeling better enough to worry about how she looks these days. Honestly!"

"Alley, I just came from checking on our house, and I'm too tired to go back tonight. It will have to wait for tomorrow. I'm sorry. I guess it is good news," Albert said as he dropped down in the rocking chair by the door. "Wait; they were allowed to see her, and I haven't been told I could go back down yet?"

"Don't split hairs, Albert! Just be glad we got some good news. I think there are a couple dresses in that bag you packed for her in a hurry the night you brought her here this summer. I'll take a look if you don't mind."

"Don't mind at all, Alley. Maybe I can drop them off tomorrow afternoon when my route takes me close to Augusta." Albert pulled himself up out of the rocking chair and he lumbered out of the room. He'd tell the boys their mother was feeling better. They'd be pleased if they even remembered who she was at this point.

Chapter Thirty-One

Albert looked in the bag Alley had given him that morning to take down to the hospital for Gracie. He loved Alley, but these dresses were not appropriate for the hospital, especially in November. What was he even thinking about when he'd packed them to bring to Alley's boarding house? He wasn't thinking, of course. His stomach still churned when he pulled up the memory of that night. Oh well; he'd have to stop by the Bassett Road mid-way through his bakery route. It shouldn't take him too long to go through her things in their bedroom and pick a couple dresses. *Lord knows, Gracie never had much for clothes. We couldn't afford it, and she was used to making do with what she had. Maybe too used to making do,* Albert thought.

Albert shook himself after he opened their bedroom door and looked around for Gracie's things. He didn't understand why something like this should be bothering him so much. She had been at the hospital now for two months. He should be able to handle this small task, but his stomach was in knots. Damn it all, he was going to have to take a trip to their outhouse.

Back in the bedroom minutes later, Albert's eyes settled on their bed. He had never bothered to make it after leaving to go to Alley's house. *Too late now.* Albert looked over the dresses Gracie had hanging on a hook by their bed. Heavens, these house dresses in the front were so worn out. Frayed along the neckline, some of them. Why hadn't he noticed this before? He dug deeper into the dresses for something that looked a little better. He stopped when he had his hands on a blue and white dress. This one looked okay. Gracie hadn't worn it in quite a while. Maybe because of a little baby fat after having Stevie. She could certainly fit into it now. She had lost so much weight just before going into the hospital. Albert yanked the garment off its hanger. He froze when he saw the dress underneath it. It was the white and gray one with embroidery on the front.

Gracie had that dress on the day Albert first spied her at church camp. Little wisp of a thing. Couldn't have weighed more than a hundred pounds, but she was so cute. Massive blue eyes. Wispy, childlike curls around her face. The way she frowned at him when he approached her and then grinned as she was turning away. God, he loved that Gracie! Where had she gone? That was only seven or eight years ago.

Albert told himself to get a grip. His bread needed to be delivered. He needed to do his job to get paid. He grabbed a couple other dresses that had been hanging behind the "church camp" dress and walked out of the room with the three of them. He considered himself lucky that Stella hadn't noticed his truck and walked over to check on him. What in God's name had he been thinking getting involved with her? Again, he hadn't been.

Later that day Albert walked into the hospital with the clothing he had brought for Gracie. He planned to leave them at the desk with instructions and run back to work, but the receptionist caught him off guard when she asked him to wait a few minutes to see a nurse. He paced back and forth in front of the reception desk.

"Mr. Grant, thanks for waiting. Do you remember me? I'm Miss Downer. I work with your wife," said the young woman who appeared.

"Yes, of course. I mean, I do remember you from a previous visit." Albert tried to smile now. "Please call me Albert."

"Albert, we're so sorry about that other visit. It was just too soon. Gracie's doctor feels she's doing better now and would benefit from a visit with you. Would it be possible for you to come see her sometime soon?"

"Well, I guess so. Is she asking for me or the boys?" Albert rolled his Harris Bakery hat into a tight lump with both hands.

"Why, I think she is about ready to ask about her family, Albert. It's always hard for a patient who has been as ill as Gracie to approach the real world again. I'm sure she thinks about you."

"Okay, when should I plan to come down?" This pretty little nurse was hard to say no to, in Albert's opinion. "Is the weekend okay?"

"The weekend would be perfect. Shall I tell Gracie to expect you this Sunday?"

Albert agreed to the plans Miss Downer proposed, said a quick goodbye, and ran for the door. Once in his truck, he paused to worry about what he had promised. He sat gripping the steering wheel with his hands at proper driving position. He noticed the time on his watch and turned his truck on immediately. Some bread deliveries would be late today.

Chapter Thirty-Two

The traffic woke Albert up on Sunday morning. He had managed to roll over and go back to sleep after waking at four o'clock like he always did, thanks to years of his father rousing him at that time every morning to help on the farm. It still seemed early, so he wondered who was traveling down the Bassett Road. He reached over and patted the other side of the bed. *Gracie?* Damn, he remembered where he was now. He was in the city on Boutelle Avenue. He'd been there for a couple months. How foolish of him to forget! Even though Alley had diligently changed the sheets several times, Albert still smelled Gracie's scent in the bed. *Must be the pillow.*

Albert's musings were interrupted by a mumbling noise coming from the corner of the room. He rolled on his side and peered over at the iron crib jammed in the right-hand side of the tiny attic bedroom. His two-and-a-half-year-old son was once again tucked in with his baby brother. Both were stirring in the morning light. Still asleep but starting to wake. Wayne's blond curls pressed against baby Steve's bald noggin, his arm placed protectively over Steve's back. Albert smiled as he gazed at his offspring. Wayne had a bed in the younger foster children's room on the other side of the attic, but he preferred this, obviously.

A cry of "Albert!" and a firm knock on the bedroom door brought him out of his dozing state. "You wanted me to wake you up this morning for your trip down to see Gracie," Mrs. Alley said, and she pounded down the hall to wake up the kids in the other bedroom with a less-than-gentle screech. Crying and jabbering were heard coming down the hall now.

"Daddy, baby's awake," announced Wayne, peeking through the slats of the crib.

"And Waynie, too," replied Albert. He smiled at both of them. "Hi, Poopa," he cooed at Stevie. As he approached the crib, they both stood up.

"Can I go, too?" asked Wayne.

"Go where, Critter?" said Albert.

"See Mommy."

"No, son, only Daddy can go today. Mommy's very sick."

"Too sick for us," said Waynie to his baby brother. Albert froze at their crib side.

Gracie rolled over on her cot that Sunday morning. She had rolled and rolled all night. She couldn't stop thinking about those dresses Albert brought to the hospital. Did he think if he brought that church camp dress to her she would turn into his "sweet" Gracie again? Then the angel in her head scolded her about wearing it to please him and make everyone think she is better. "Smarten up and act sane, you idiot," said Gracie to herself. Heads turned her way, and she realized she had said that out loud. She smiled. "Sorry." Heads turned away. Breakfast was announced, thank goodness.

Gracie looked at herself as best she could in the mirror over the sink in the bathroom of the ward. She had washed up and put on the dress from her first meeting with Albert at church camp years ago. *Damned thing fits with room to spare*, she thought. She had lost so much weight. *I look like the half-starved daughter of the town drunk again.*

"Gracie? Are you in there?" said a familiar voice.

"Yes, Miss Downer," replied Gracie.

"I think it is time you called me Dena. We're friends, aren't we? Just don't call me Dena in front of old Mrs. Wight. She would not approve. Maybe not in front of other patients either. Okay?"

"I guess so."

"And I love this dress on you! Gracie, you are a pretty thing! What can I do to help?"

Gracie smiled now. "What can I do with my hair? Look at this mop! Plus, I have no lipstick."

"It's a good thing you have me, Gracie." Dena pulled her purse out from behind her back. "You know I love to fix ladies up." She placed her purse on the side of the sink and started rummaging through it. Gracie relaxed and let herself enjoy being helped. In a few minutes, both Dena and she smiled at the new and improved image of Gracie they saw reflecting back at them.

"Dena, I'm nervous about this," said Gracie, turning to the nurse.

"My dear, he is probably just as nervous as you are after what happened at his last visit. How about you pretend this is a blind date, and you look at him with fresh eyes. Like you don't even know him."

"Shit. You are something else, you know that?" But Gracie grinned and petted the nurse on one shoulder. Dena wrapped her arms around Gracie for a big hug.

"Gracie, I don't understand all that landed you in this place, but you are the brightest light I have worked with in this hospital. I want you to get better and get out of here."

"Me, too, Dena. Me, too!"

Albert was standing back to the door that Gracie and Dena used to enter the visitors' lounge. Gracie noticed right away that his suit was huge on him. He had lost weight, too. *As if he could afford to.* He was a slight fellow to begin with. Feather-weight boxer. *Golden gloves, my Albert was.* When he turned around, Gracie stared at that round, baby face of his. 'Look at him as if you don't know him,' Dena had said. This guy looked like a kid. Gracie smiled at him.

Albert burst into a broad grin. "Hi, Gracie. You look gorgeous!"

The two of them sat side-by-side on a couch. Neither of them spoke for a while. Miss Downer had officially left, but she was peeking at them from just outside the door where she hoped they wouldn't notice her. When Gracie reached over and touched Albert's hand, Miss Downer smiled and turned to leave.

"Waynie says hello," Albert searched his wife's face now.

"How are the boys?" asked Gracie.

"They're okay, but they miss you." Albert now took Gracie's hand in his.

"Stevie probably doesn't even remember me."

"Oh, I think he might if he saw you again." Albert stared at his shoes.

They sat quietly for another few minutes. Holding hands. Looking at everything but each other. Then Albert babbled about his work at the bakery. Gracie smiled and acted like she was listening. Head Nurse Wight came into the lounge and announced that visiting hours were over.

Albert jumped up, almost pulling Gracie over with the hand he still held.

"Goodbye, Gracie. Take care." Albert pecked Gracie on the cheek and turned quickly to find the door. He was gone. Gracie stood looking at the door he escaped through.

"Gracie, how did it go?" asked Miss Downer's sweet voice when she caught up with Gracie in the hall a few minutes later.

"Your advice was perfect, Dena. I don't know that man who was just here."

Gracie let the nurse walk her back to the ward.

Chapter Thirty-Three

Albert arrived back at Boutelle Avenue earlier than Mrs. Alley thought he would, and he caught a sight and overhead words not intended for his eyes and ears. Mrs. Alley's face reddened when she turned and saw him standing inside the back door.

"Al, I'm sorry about that," Mrs. Alley sputtered as she watched him grab his Stevie out of the arms of the foster girl who'd been playing with him instead of doing her chores. The girl used the opportunity to escape the room and Mrs. Alley's scolding.

"It's okay, Alley. I know Stevie's been fussy lately, and he's a real burden for you," replied Albert as he settled in his favorite spot in the kitchen—the rocking chair—with his son. "Waynie fits in and plays with the kids, but this little, rock-headed character has always been a handful."

Mrs. Alley put her hands to the sides of her face and sighed. "He just misses his mother."

"I'll bring him up to my sister Ruth's this Saturday, Alley. My next visit down to the hospital is not until two more Sundays."

"No, Al… I thought you said you didn't want her to get her clutches on him 'cause she wouldn't want to let go, and her husband is so starved for a son, you might have to fight him to get Stevie back."

"All the same, Alley, he's too much for you. She'll be thrilled to have him." Albert closed his eyes and rested his cheek against Stevie's bald noggin. With his mind drifting, he half-listened as Mrs. Alley went through the supper routine with all the kids in the next room. He startled and almost lost grip of Stevie when he felt hands on his thighs.

"Daddy, baby was fussy!" announced Wayne from his stance between his dad's knees. "Mom was mad."

"Mom?" said Albert. His heart gave a slight squeeze. "Oh, you mean Mrs. Alley?"

"Yeah, Mrs. Alley. That mom." Wayne grinned at him, and turned and dashed off to join the crowd of kids helping to get the table ready for supper.

Mrs. Alley came rushing through the kitchen on her way to a pot on the stove and paused.

"Al, why don't you put that baby down and take a rest yourself before supper? You look worn out, kid."

"Alley, Wayne calls you 'Mom' now. Do you notice?"

"Al, they all call me 'Mom.' He just mimics the foster kids. Don't worry about it."

"I don't know if he will even remember his mother when she's well again. If she gets well again, that is." Albert groaned as he moved out of the rocker with Stevie on his chest. "This babe isn't missing any meals, is he? He's as rugged as Wayne is willowy. Gracie will be a stranger to Stevie. Should I take Wayne up to Ruth's farm, too, Alley? Would give you more of a break."

"Ask him, Al. If he wants to stay here, he's no trouble. The kids love him." Mrs. Alley leaned over and kissed the top of Stevie's head. "Ruth might find this one enough at first. Did you talk about Wayne to Ruth, too?"

"No," sighed Albert.

"Leave him here then. Go put that one down and come have some supper in a bit. Wayne's not the only scrawny Grant male in this house."

"Yes, ma'am," whispered Albert as he walked past Mrs. Alley and toward the stairs.

After supper, Albert sat in the living room watching both Mrs. Alley and her husband sleep on the couch. The house was quiet except for some giggling girls in the bedroom off the front hall. Albert decided they must know that the Alleys are always asleep on the sofa by this time of night. He had a half a mind to sneak over to their door and rap on it to scare them, but he thought better of it. Alley would probably snatch him bald for causing a stir this time of night. Instead he thought again of the possibility that his young wife might not get better enough to come home to him and the boys. What would he do then? He even went as far as wondering what kind of mother Stella would be.

"Get that thought out of your head, Grantie," muttered Albert to himself. But he couldn't get the thought of Stella out of his mind completely. He carefully got up out of his chair and tiptoed to the front door. He glanced back at the sleeping couple. Not a stir. *Wouldn't hurt to drive over to the Bassett Road to see what Stella is up to tonight. Beautiful evening for a drive. Even in that damned old bakery truck. Maybe her husband is out of town.* That last thought cheered Albert up enough to smile.

Chapter Thirty-Four

Dr. Knowles waited patiently for Gracie to speak. He thought she seemed unsettled after the weekend visit with her husband. Finally giving in, he asked, "How did your visit with Albert go yesterday?"

"That man is a stranger to me," replied Gracie without even looking at the doctor.

"He's probably uncomfortable with you, too," answered the doctor.

Gracie sat quietly and stared out the office window. Dr. Knowles stirred in his chair and shuffled a few file folders on his desk, and then spoke again. "Gracie, did you have contact with any of your siblings, or were they too far away?"

"No more Albert talk?"

"Not for now, Gracie. We still need to sort out your childhood. Albert will have to wait."

Gracie smiled. She liked that idea. "I saw my sisters some as I was growing up. Flippie was taken in by a wonderful family in Dover. God, they spoiled her rotten. Her foster mother used to box up her clothes after she outgrew them and send them down to me."

"Was nice of her. Did you ever meet the lady?"

"Yep, I did. A few times she sent my mother tickets for us to ride to Dover on the Narrow Gauge."

"Wait, the what?"

"Doc, you really are an outta-stater." Now Gracie giggled.

"So, clue this poor doctor in then, Gracie." Dr. Knowles put both elbows on his desk and leaned in a bit to listen.

"The Narrow Gauge was what we traveled on when I was a kid. Jeez, I still miss it. It was like a mini version of the regular train. My little brother loved it. Was just his size. Mrs. Witham would send us tickets in the mail, and we would travel from Augusta to Dover. She and Mr. Witham would pick us up there. We'd stay overnight. They treated Flippie like she was their own daughter. Was really something. Once or twice, I saw Cora up there, too, but my older sister wasn't so lucky. One of Mrs. Witham's relatives took her in for a while, but they kept sending her back to the orphanage. She bounced all around. Cora and I were jealous of Flippie, I guess. Foolish, wasn't it? Not her fault she lucked out."

"How about your brother? Kenneth, was it?"

"Hah!" Gracie looked down and rubbed her face. When she looked back up, she blurted, "Kenneth was a two-year-old boy, I said boy, when he was taken. Everyone wants a boy, you know. He was officially adopted right away, so the rest of us never saw him."

"Have you ever seen him as an adult?"

"Once," whispered Gracie, now with her head down again. "He was eighteen and going off to war and old enough to make his own decisions."

Dr. Knowles watched Gracie and waited.

"Sent me a letter at my uncle's house in Winslow. Asked me to meet him at the Waterville bus station. I didn't even want to go at first, but Uncle Polly kept pestering me about 'how would I feel if he was killed in action' and all that. So, I went."

Dr. Knowles beat out a rhythm with his index fingers on his desk as he waited rather impatiently for Gracie to continue.

"All right, all right, so I knew him right away. Some of his buddies were getting off the bus with him, and they all laughed about how I was a pretty version of him in a skirt. Had a few other comments that aren't worth repeating. Fool Kenneth stood there grinning ear to ear. Didn't have a damned thing to say to me, but it was good to finally see him. He was cute in his uniform. He wrote to me from overseas." Gracie smiled at her hands. "He's a nice guy."

"Did he survive the war, Gracie?"

"Yes, I hear he's married with a baby girl. Flippie wants to have a reunion of the siblings at her camp in Abbott, well, the Witham's camp.

All she could babble about when she visited me this summer. That and me not taking care of myself. How could she understand the stuff that Cora and I have gone through? She has no right to scold me. No right!"

Gracie held her left hand to her face, covering her scar. She started to rock slightly.

"Gracie, you know you're safe here. I won't tell these people what you're sharing with me. Can you tell me about one of your visits to Dover?"

"One time, I was about eleven 'cause Ira John was three that summer, so Flippie was fourteen years old. Had quite the figure and everything. I slept with her in her bed after a long tub supervised by Mrs. Witham, so I wouldn't soil anything, you see. In the morning, Flippie got up and put just her underwear on and went parading out in the hall like that. Startled me to death! Couldn't do something like that at our house in Windsor if the old man was home. No, sir! He'd have had at her, for sure!"

Gracie paused and caught her breath. "But Mr. Witham just laughed and told her to go get her clothes on. She wouldn't have survived in Windsor. She sure wouldn't." Now Gracie rocked more vigorously.

Dr. Knowles watched her for a minute and let her calm down. "Gracie, you have good reason to have been envious of your sister Flippie. Your situations couldn't have been more extremely different. You also need to understand that she has no way of understanding what you have been through. It's a wonder you have any relationship at all."

Gracie glanced up at the doctor. "No one ever gave me that right, Doc. I was always told to be thankful for the visits to Dover and grateful for all those damned, hand-me-down clothes."

"You have my permission to be angry, Gracie. Okay?"

"Okay, Doc. I'm really tired. Are we done for today?"

"Done for today, Gracie, but with lots more to talk about soon."

Chapter Thirty-Five

Gracie rolled over on her cot in the ward and muttered about the noisy women she had to share her world with at this damned hospital. The crying didn't stop, though. It was then that she noticed the tone of the voice was familiar. *Cheryl Lee?* Gracie peered around. No attendants in the immediate area. She sneaked out of her bed and looked over at where Cheryl Lee's bed was. *It is her crying. Damn!* Gracie had not interacted much with the poor thing since she'd lost her library job for her. She approached Cheryl Lee's cot anyway.

"Cheryl, what's the matter?" she whispered as she knelt by her pillow.

Cheryl Lee sniffled and glared at Gracie. "Well, if it isn't Miss Prissy herself. You talking to me again?" Her tearful yet pouty expression was childlike, as usual.

"Sorry to bother you. Just heard you crying," said Gracie.

"Never you mind about me, Gracie. I can do without your high and mighty shit."

Gracie started to get up to return to bed when Cheryl Lee looked up and gasped. The night attendant Gus loomed over them at the foot of the cot.

"You say anything about anything, little bitch, and you'll fucking regret it," he hissed. "And you get out of here, too, damn you! This was directed at Gracie. "Dr. Knowles' pet patient."

Gracie scrambled back to her cot and covered up even her head and lay gasping as quietly as she could. She listened for Gus' footsteps, but they did not bring him near. He went toward the ward door instead. There was no snoring to be heard now. All patients were holding their breaths it seemed.

Morning finally came to the ward. Gracie couldn't remember how long she had been awake shivering in the night. As she sat up, she looked for Cheryl Lee.

"Ladies! Ladies! Did everyone oversleep?" hollered Nurse Wight as she charged through the ward. "Up with all of you, or you'll miss breakfast!"

The ward patients glanced at one another. Not a word was spoken about the night before. Gracie felt her heart break as she readied herself for the day. The first patient out the ward door was Cheryl Lee.

Chapter Thirty-Six

"Hey, donut man!" Stella shook Albert awake. "Time to finish your deliveries."

"Oh, geez, I am tired," moaned Albert. "Wake me up in ten minutes." He rolled over on Stella's yellow flowered sheets. "I'll just snooze in your garden, here."

"What?"

"Never seen flowered sheets before." Albert yawned and rolled away from Stella.

"Al, what are we doing here?" Stella leaned over Albert. She was already dressed. Albert's black shoes, white socks, brown bakery uniform, and white underwear were scattered on her bedroom floor, in that order.

"What do you mean, what are we doing here? You haven't exactly fought me off here, Stel."

Stella stood, arms akimbo, by the bed now. "Doesn't mean I don't have a troubled conscience about what I'm doing with you. You never say how Gracie's doing. Once in a while you show up with those tow-headed babies to remind me she exists. Never ask about Silas and me, either."

"We don't exactly talk much," said Albert as he sat himself up against a pillow.

"No, we don't. Do you even wonder why I'm not faithful to my husband?"

"Just figured your Silas was unavailable to you, Stel. Just in a different way than Gracie is to me."

Stella sat back down on the side of the bed again. "Damn, Al, you somehow read me pretty well, don't you?"

"And you me, Stel," whispered Albert as he leaned in to kiss her.

She rebuffed him and jumped up again. "Well, I'm getting afraid that Silas will find out about us. He has enough problems without this. We need to stop doing this. Now!"

Stella walked out of the bedroom. Albert could hear her moving pots and pans around in her tiny Betty-Crocker-decorated kitchen. He got up and started gathering his clothing. He dressed quickly and went to say goodbye. He found Stella, head bowed, crying into her sink. She refused to look at him to say goodbye. She blurted out, "Please don't come back, Al. Don't. This can't go anywhere."

Albert sneaked out Stella's back door and into his own backyard as he had always done, so Bunny Cates wouldn't have a chance to see him sneak over to where he had parked in his own driveway. He plunked into the driver's seat of his bakery truck. *Damn*, thought Albert, *these rendezvous were about the only thing keeping me going in all this mess! Now what?*

"You know what, asshole," Albert said out loud to himself as he tried to start his truck. "Deliver bread and donuts to North Vassalboro. Make some money to keep this messed up life afloat."

Damned truck wouldn't turn over after three tries. Albert pounded the steering wheel and pumped the clutch. The fourth try found the vehicle hardly making a sound. Albert jumped out and slammed the door shut. He kicked the front tire on the driver's side so fiercely he hurt his right foot. Crumbling onto the truck running board, he started to cry as he pulled off his shoe and rubbed his foot. He cowered now to hide his tears as he feared a neighbor might see him. When he did look up, he spied Stella looking at him out her side window. She moved from the window as soon as she noticed him looking back. Albert got up and, favoring his right foot, got back into the truck and waited for it to recover from being flooded. He eventually got it started and went about his delivery.

Chapter Thirty-Seven

Miss Downer found Gracie in the hall. "Gracie, aren't you going to Dr. Knowles' office for your session?" Gracie didn't answer. She didn't even look up. "Gracie, what's wrong with you today?"

"Well, my dear friend Dena, let me ask you a question, please." Gracie finally said.

"What is it, Gracie? Why the tone, by the way?"

"If Cheryl Lee is telling lies about being molested or worse around here, why is that creepy night attendant Gus threatening her?"

Miss Downer plunked beside Gracie and fiddled with her class ring. "Gracie, when did you hear about this?"

"I didn't just hear about it. I actually heard him threaten her. And he called me Dr. Knowles' pet patient. Why?"

"Dr. Knowles has scolded the attendants about their treatment of you. He considers you salvageable. Probably more correct to say that you're his pet project. Is that bad?"

"No, but how about Cheryl Lee?"

Now Miss Downer took her time answering. Gracie glared at her. Finally she replied, "I don't know the answer to that." They sat for a minute. The nurse took Gracie's left hand in hers. "Gracie, please, go to your session. Say you're sorry you were late. Don't bring up Cheryl Lee. You've come so damned far. Do you really want to risk everything for something you have no control over?"

"What the hell kind of answer is that?" snapped Gracie as she yanked her hand away.

"It's the only answer I have for you right now. Honestly, I know bad things sometimes happen around here, especially at night. I'll ask around and see if I can find out what Gus was talking about, but please, Gracie, go to your session. Do you want to get out of here or not? Do you want to see your little boys again?"

Gracie sighed. "Of course, I want to get out of this place and see my boys. I don't understand how you can stand to work here, though. You must see things. Is there anyone you can talk to?"

"Maybe, Gracie. Please get going. Think about yourself, please. I'll see what I can do for Cheryl Lee."

Gracie knocked on Dr. Knowles' office door and went in when he invited her. "I'm sorry I'm late, Doc." She bit her lip.

"You don't look too sorry. Everything okay?"

Gracie glanced at the doctor for a minute. "Women problems."

"Great, Gracie!"

"Huh?"

"Not to be too indiscrete, Gracie, but if that is happening for you then your body is recovering. It's good news, believe me."

Gracie thought somehow it was all too easy, but she went with it. She even tried to look embarrassed. Nurse Downer's words rang in her head, and she pushed thoughts of last night away and asked the doctor about the agenda.

"Shall I tell you more about my siblings, Doc?"

"Yes, Gracie, but I'm also interested in finding out if you remember not talking for a period of time in your childhood, too."

"How did you know I did that?"

"Just guessing. Can you tell me about such a time?"

"Well, the first time I can think of involved my mother's death. Before that, I would just hide in daydreams, you know, especially if my mom and I had to stay in with neighbors because the old man had taken off and left us without wood to keep warm. People wouldn't be all that kind to us. Made us work hard for a meal and a spot on their floor. I used to tell myself to 'hide in my head,' you see."

"That's a common reaction to a difficult situation, even with adults, Gracie."

"Maybe. Got harder to do when Ira John came along. I had to watch him like a hawk when we were in other people's houses. Little Christer would get into things." Gracie paused and laughed softly. "He's probably causing problems now. He's still just a kid."

"How old?"

"Oh, he's fifteen now. Giving Aunt Edie and Uncie a hell of a time in Windsor, I'm sure. He still goes and pesters the old man. Drunken Kent likes him. He lets him drive his old junk cars. Tells me things like, 'Gracie, Dad's just a harmless old drunk.' Jesus, I guess it's easy to forget bad memories that happened before you were four years old, especially if the really horrible things didn't happen to you personally. Well, Al and I try to take him in our house in Winslow when we can. I try to knock some sense into his head. Well, I did until recently." Gracie hung her head.

"Gracie, what changed when your mother died?"

Gracie looked up at Dr. Knowles. "I did, Doc. Was sick of everything and everybody. Didn't know what to say to people when they badgered me with questions, and then after a while everyone got used to me not talking. I stayed in my bed and refused to talk or eat. Most people left me alone except for Aunt Lucy. She was missing my work around the house, you see. Grandpa John told her to leave me alone to my grief, but she kept sneaking into my bedroom and goading me."

"Goading you how?"

"Threatening to send me away to another family member if I couldn't work for my supper. When that didn't work, she called me crazy and threatened to have me sent to 'one of those places where they lock you up and throw away the key because you're nuts.' Foolish Frenchie didn't know the name of a place like this. Surprised she had the courage to come visit me here. Probably didn't want people thinking I was completely over the edge. Wanted to be able to tell them I could have visitors and all."

"How did things finally change, Gracie?"

"Oh, that's quite the story, Doc."

"Gracie, can you just tell me as yourself without the usual performance, please?"

"Thought you enjoyed my storytelling, Doc?"

Dr. Knowles smiled. "I do, but I'd like to hear this from you and not the story teller, please." He waited for her to speak.

"If I just tell you straight, Doc, I'll get angry and cry."

"I can handle your anger and your tears. Okay?"

Gracie sat and looked at the doctor for a moment. "That's how it involved my siblings, you see. I was sixteen when my mother died. My sisters Flippie and Cora showed up. Never did find out who called them in to have at me. Probably Uncle Polly. He must have gotten tired of his damned wife fussing at him. I was lying on my bed just floating. It was the only way I didn't feel too much pain."

Dr. Knowles interrupted Gracie. "What do you mean by floating?"

"I don't know, Doc, just staying in my head, I guess, and ignoring everything and everybody. It feels like I'm above my body, so I think that's why I call it floating."

"Can you hear people around you when you do this, Gracie?"

"Only if I want to hear them. Usually I go in and out as far as listening goes. So, I was floating, and suddenly I spy Flippie's face over mine. Her mouth was going a mile a minute, but I had turned her off. Poor Flippie. I hadn't noticed she was talking to someone else, too. Suddenly, I was grabbed by my shoulders and shaken really hard. Then Cora's face was in mine.

'Cut this fucking shit out, Grace Elnora!' she snapped. She was really hard to ignore. That gruff voice and her WAC swearing. Jeezum, Doc. She was horrible with that."

"WAC?"

"Women's Army Corp. Cora went in as soon as she could to get away from some of the nasty living situations she'd been put in. She was a force to be reckoned with before she went in, but she was something else after a couple years in there."

"So you stopped floating at that point, I take it."

"No choice. Had to stop floating. She told me I would consider where I was living a dream come true compared to some of the shit holes she had had to put up with when she was my age. Told me I had to smarten up. She and Flippie were there to get me ready to go to our mother's funeral in Cooper's Mills. She had been given a leave to do so and wasn't going to waste her time playing games with me. I did ask both of them what they were doing there. Didn't realize they would care whether or not they went to Myrabelle Murray's funeral. Flippie just laughed nervously, but Cora let me have it again.

'You think you're the only one who considered her your mother? I never had a mother after the God damned town took me away. Flippie here had Mrs. Witham. Sweet lady, she was, but not her friggin' sister who would take me in for a while then send me back to the orphanage if the damned bitch felt like it. I'd get sent to some foster home that wanted slave labor. Mrs. Witham would fuss at her sister about me not being in a decent place, and she would take me back for a while, especially if the house needed spring cleaning.' Flippie tried to interrupt her, but Cora paid no attention to her and continued to tell me, 'Myrabelle was the only mother I ever had, even if I was only with her for five years. I'm going to her funeral, and so are you two, so there.'

Cora and Flippie yanked me around getting me dressed. Thought Cora was going to pull all my hair out trying to fix it. Uncle Polly drove us down to Cooper's Mills. We three girls—well Cora was twenty one by then and Flippie nineteen—but anyway, we all sat in the back seat. Grandpa John rode shotgun. Cora had at him, too, as we drove along.

She said, 'What the hell were you thinking telling this young girl that our mother died of an asthma attack?' He told her he thought that's what happened. 'Her heart gave out, you old fool!' Cora told him. 'What were you thinking filling her head with ideas like that?' Grandpa refused to talk to her anymore.

We got to the cemetery, and who do we see standing there big as Billy Be Damned next to Aunt Bernice and Aunt Georgette? Kent Murray. Someone had cleaned him up and put him in a suit, for God's sake. It was a quick graveside service, and we turned to go. Aunt Georgette ran over and stopped us saying that Aunt Bernice insisted we come over and say hello to our father. Flippie just looked startled at the idea, but the look on Cora's face! Uncle Polly and Grandpa had gone ahead to get the car started. They had been damned uncomfortable during the whole thing, you see." Gracie stopped and caught her breath. "I'm sorry, Doc. I seem to have fallen into a story again."

"It's okay, Gracie. You've got me hooked. Finish the cemetery scene, please, and then we'll just talk."

"So, I waited for Cora to sound off and then some, but she didn't. She looked up at Aunt Bernice just as the pious old lady commanded that we come over. Cora grabbed both Flippie and me and walked us all toward her. We all stood there looking the old man over. He said nothing to us. Aunt Bernice told Cora to kiss her father's hand. She even pulled it up toward her. Heavens, I was nervous. Just then we heard Ira John hollering for us. He scampered across the cemetery hell-bent for us. He was eight at that point. Aunt Edie was coming up behind him explaining that she was sorry they missed the service but Ira John wanted to see his sisters, so they came just the same. We turned and hugged the both of them and left Aunt Bernice holding her brother's hand. When we did finally look back at them, they were making their way to Aunt Bernice's fancy car.

'Good riddance,' hissed Cora. 'Old bastard can rot in hell as far as I'm concerned.'

It was then I decided I was back out, Doc. I had Cora to lean on and Flippie to help her. Went back to Winslow, my sisters had a meal with us and took the bus back up to Guilford, and Aunt Lucy asked me to wash up the dishes. Life went on, I guess."

There was silence for a minute or two. Gracie fussed at the front of her dress while Dr. Knowles just looked at her.

"Gracie, what would you say to Cora and Flippie if you could go back in time to the day of your mother's funeral?"

Gracie wrapped one arm around herself, held the left side of her face with the hand of the other arm, and rocked gently back and forth in her chair. "It's too much, just too much," whispered Gracie.

"What's too much, Gracie? Please tell me."

"This whole friggin' family, that's what!"

"Continue, Gracie."

"Everything is messed up. No one cares what others are putting up with, and everyone is jealous of everyone else, and I'm just supposed to keep my mouth shut and put up with all this shit!" Gracie was sobbing in an odd controlled way now and still rocking.

"Continue…"

"All I do is work and wait on everyone and no one gives one damn, Doc!"

"Sometimes it seems like that, Gracie."

"All the time, Doc. I was smart, you know. If I had had someone to help me, I could have been more than just a slave housewife, you know. I hate everything in my life, hate it!"

Dr. Knowles came around his desk and handed Gracie a handkerchief from his pocket. He sat on the front of his desk now.

"You must think I'm awful, Doc. I mean, I don't really hate my boys, but they are so much work all the time. I don't have a car. Don't even have a driver's license. Can't get away from the house if I wanted to go somewhere."

"I know you don't hate the people in your life, Gracie. You hate all the bad things that have happened to you. The people were all just part of it. These things are what you need to sort out."

"How in God's name could I ever sort out this mess, Doc?"

Dr. Knowles smiled at his patient. "We'll do it, Gracie. We will. You are very smart and with my help, we'll do it."

At that point, Gracie blew her nose loudly. Dr. Knowles was startled.

"My mother used to say that I'd blow my brains out the way I honk my nose." They both laughed. "Doc, do you know there are things going on in this hospital that shouldn't be going on?"

"I do know that, Gracie."

"Really?"

"Really, Gracie, but you need to leave that stuff for us to work on and worry about getting yourself better."

Gracie got up to leave. She paused at the office door and glanced back at Dr. Knowles as he was shuffling folders. *I wonder if he does really know.*

Chapter Thirty-Eight

This notorious Waterville bar was a place Albert had never seen the insides of, even though as a teen he'd been by it several times on the way to a fight with the Lebanese boys who lived just down from it at the head of the falls of the Kennebec River. As he sat in front of a beer at the dark bar of the Bob-In with Phil Dunn and a few others from the bakery that Friday afternoon, he felt guilty.

"Jesus, Grantie, lighten up," said Phil as he poked at Albert with his left elbow. He took a long swig from the glass in his other hand and let out a loud belch. "It's not like Gracie will find out you're here, for Christ's sake."

"I know, Phil, I know. It's just that I probably should be home with the boys now," replied Albert. He glanced around and noticed men dressed in Harris Bakery uniforms toasting the end of the work week. He held his glass aloft for a few seconds and then took a drink.

The second beer went down easier. Albert found himself laughing at the stupid jokes being told. He did feel a bit lighter now. He ordered a third for himself and offered to pay for one for Phil, too. The two of them decided to sit down at a table.

"How you holding up, Al?" Phil shouted in Albert's ear above the din of the little hole-in-the-wall drinking establishment.

"God, Phil, I don't know what I'm going to do if I can't get Gracie home soon. I'm scared."

"She doing any better?"

"Some, but she's got a ways to go, I guess. The doctor would like me to come down and take her out of the hospital for an outing. Last time I saw her she was in no mood to go anywhere with me. He claims she's better. I don't know."

Phil put his hand on Albert's shoulder and said, "I don't know anything about this stuff, Al. I'd follow the doctor's orders, I guess. By the way, are you still visiting that pretty, little neighbor of yours, you old dog?"

"Listen, Phil, keep your damned voice down. Where did you hear anything about that?"

"Al, did you really think you were going to fool Bunny Cates by sneaking around the back of those tiny Bassett Road houses?"

"What the hell?" Albert slammed his beer glass down and half of the contents decorated the thighs of his pants. "Oh, great! I'm going back to Alley's for supper smelling like a brewery."

"Take it easy, buddy," said Phil as he handed Albert his handkerchief to help him sop up the beer. "It's not like Bunny's gonna go down to Augusta and tell on you. She can't drive, and her lazy, supposedly ill husband wouldn't get off the couch long enough to take her."

"Yuh, well, that ship has sailed, Phil," said Albert, holding the soggy handkerchief over the edge of the table in an effort to air dry it.

"No way, Al."

"Stel's afraid Silas will find out. What the hell?!"

"Women! Damn them all!" Phil chugged the rest of his drink. "You need another beer to replace that one, Al. My turn to buy." He jumped up.

Albert didn't finish his fourth beer. He was a light-weight drinker, and it took him forever to find his sea legs and make his way out of the Bob-In. He sat in his truck for a while and felt sorry for himself. Maybe he needed a dose of his sister Ruth. He decided to go visit her on Sunday. Wayne would be glad to see his baby brother, and Albert felt he himself could benefit from a gentle scolding from Ruth about keeping his chin up. He would have to go to church service with her, but even that sounded comforting to him in the blue mood he was in. He decided to munch down a few leftover donuts to soak up the alcohol. After two plain ones, Albert decided he could drive the short distance up to Boutelle Avenue. Old Alley wouldn't notice anything different about him, would she?

Ruth's farm at Livermore was chilly that Sunday afternoon. Her husband hadn't gotten around to chopping any of the large logs stacked by the shed. Albert decided he would do enough to at least get Ruth by for a week or so. Chopping each log gave Albert a chance to vent some frustration. He pounded harder and harder with each blow. When he took a break to create a stack by the back door, he noticed Ruth watching him.

"Anything you want to cry on your sister's shoulder about there, kid?" asked Ruth. She gave Albert that knowing look of hers. "Going pretty hard at that wood."

Albert finished stacking the last few pieces he had lugged over to the door and looked up at his sister. "I just don't know what to do, Ruthie. Just don't. Don't know my ass from a hole in the ground lately."

"Care to explain that a little simpler?" Ruth motioned at Albert to sit down on the porch swing with her.

Albert set down shoulder to shoulder with Ruth, but he didn't look at her. The porch swing sang to them as it rocked to and fro.

"Either we slow down this swing and you start talking Al, or I'll be sick. What's going on?"

Albert plunked his feet down and looked up at Ruth. "Sis, you know I haven't been faithful to my wedding vows since Gracie has been sick, don't you?"

"I don't want to hear about that, little brother. I want to hear what you're going to do to rectify the situation, please. Are you going to try to salvage your marriage for your boys' sake or not?"

"That's just it, Sis. I don't know if there will be anything to salvage."

"What on earth do you mean?"

"What if she doesn't get better and get out of that hospital? What then?"

Ruth reared back, turned sideways, and glared at Albert now. "You best stop talking like that, for the first thing. Secondly, you go down there and start acting like you miss that young woman and want her home, not because you need the help with the babies, but because you love her and want her. Do you hear me?"

"What if she doesn't want me anymore?"

"Albert Russell Grant, you know that little thing had experienced hard times before you married her. You actually going to tell me you plan to reject her now like everyone else in her life has done in the past?"

"No, Ruthie, I do love her, you know. It's just that I don't know if she still loves me. What about that?"

"Gracie doesn't know what end is up after what she's been through. It's up to you to show her love and understanding. You find God in your heart and do what a good man should do." Ruth gave the swing a good push now and almost rocked Albert off onto the porch floor.

"All right, all right, Sis," said Albert as he grabbed the side of the swing. Ruth and Albert swung for a few moments, both staring out at the apple orchard where Ruth's husband Junior was picking.

"Momma," hollered Albert's niece through the screen door. "That chicken smells done, but I can't get it out of the oven by myself."

Ruth stopped the swing again and looked at Albert. "Go on, Sis," he said. "I'll finish up some wood and think about what you said. Please, just don't judge me too hard."

"I'll love you no matter what, Al, but remember what Father always said: 'It's just as easy to do what's right as what's wrong.' I know you know what is right."

Albert got up after Ruth left and walked over to the wood pile. He lined up his next victim on the chopping block and thought to himself, *if father was right after all, why does it feel so good to do what's wrong? Damn.*

Chapter Thirty-Nine

Gracie and Dr. Knowles worked hard at dealing with her feelings about her siblings in the next couple of weeks, especially the older ones who had been taken from their Windsor home. The subject of Albert did eventually come back around. Dr. Knowles convinced her that a visit with Albert outside of the hospital might help her reconnect with him. She wasn't keen on the idea, but the doctor had helped her so much already. She didn't tell him that she didn't know what the word "conjugal" meant when he mentioned their visit could be of that nature if she felt comfortable with it. He had looked a bit flustered as he talked about it. Gracie decided to wait and ask Nurse Downer when she caught her back in the ward.

"Good Christ!" exclaimed Gracie as Miss Downer tried to shush her. "Is the visit supposed to help me or Albert, damn it all?"

"Gracie, maybe it will help you reconnect with your dear husband," said Miss Downer. Gracie just bit the side of her mouth and glared at her. She walked away and decided to have that battle another day.

Sunday came along before Gracie could even consider what to do about the official visit. Nurse Dena helped her get ready.

"Gracie, you are the prettiest thing!" cooed the nurse as she put a tiny amount of lipstick on Gracie and modeled rubbing her lips together for Gracie to mimic.

Gracie said nothing. She was floating now. Maybe she could get through this afternoon by doing just that. She walked down to the visitors' lounge with the nurse and a couple of other patients. He was there. That pretty baby face of his. He held his arm out to Gracie like some old church deacon seating ladies before the service. She placed her arm in his and walked out the front doors of the hospital. It was a cold November day! They stopped while she put her sweater on. Albert muttered something about remembering to bring her winter jacket down the next time he visited as he helped her into the cavernous bakery truck. They rode along the streets of Augusta with Albert occasionally chattering about things like his troubles with deliveries.

"Let's go parking like the old days, Al," said Gracie in a high, childlike voice. Albert gripped the steering wheel and looked over at her.

"You want to, Gracie?"

"Why not? Do you know of a place around here that would give us some privacy?"

"Sure, it will take us a few minutes to get there." Albert drove along, catching side glimpses of his wife as he headed out of town. When they pulled into a big gravel pit, Albert remarked, "It isn't scenic, but it's private. No one will be working here today." He shut off the truck and sat quietly. Gracie grabbed for his right hand with her left.

"Well?" she whispered as she looked in his face. Albert leaned over and kissed her. More like a peck but at least on her lips. Gracie grabbed his head and kissed him rather roughly. They both paused and started taking off necessary clothing to go further. Gracie peered down at Albert's lap.

"Well?" she said again in a more urgent fashion. She manipulated him and he responded, at least physically. She sat on his lap and gasped as he entered her.

"Okay, there?" Albert asked.

"Just get it over with," whispered Gracie.

One thrust and he was done. "God, Gracie, I'm sorry, give me a minute here."

"Never mind. We've done it. That's enough for today."

They pulled themselves together. Gracie stared right forward as Albert started the truck.

"Want to go for ice cream or something?" Albert asked as they pulled out of the gravel pit driveway. Gracie didn't answer.

Albert drove straight back to the hospital. Gracie jumped out and headed for the front door. As Albert got out and ran around the truck to help her in, she said, "What do you suppose the police are here for?" Albert hadn't noticed the two police cars.

They went inside toward the visitors' lounge but were detoured to the cafeteria. Patients were milling around where they normally were not allowed. Nurses and orderlies were trying to herd them back to wards. Gracie lost Albert somehow in the hubbub, but she noticed a fellow ward patient who could communicate fairly well, or at least better than many. Gracie made a beeline for her and caught her by the arm.

"What's going on?" Gracie asked.

She looked at Gracie with a startled expression. "Good God, Cheryl Lee was missing since lunch. Damned orderlies were running around looking everywhere for her. Guess where they finally just found the little character?"

Gracie searched her face. "Where?"

"Crazy little thing hung herself in the bathroom."

Chapter Forty

Albert sat holding Gracie like a baby in his arms. Finding her in a fetal position on the floor in the hospital foyer with people stepping over her startled him, but he gathered his wits, picked her up, and found a chair to sit down on, and there he was with his wife quietly crying into her hands. She wouldn't respond to him when he tried to talk to her. He didn't know what to do with her, so he waited and watched the drama going on around him. A gurney with a body bag ran over his toes. The orderly pushing it never stopped to say sorry as he hurried by. Nurses were fussing at patients and each other.

"Should we call one of the doctors?"

"Get these patients back to the wards, for God's sake!"

"Albert! Albert! We need to take Gracie, please." Albert looked up and noticed Nurse Downer in front of him.

"What?" He clung to his wife now, scared.

"We need to take Gracie," Nurse Downer paused and then said more emphatically, "This has obviously upset her. We need to take her now and give her some medication. Please help this orderly put her on the gurney."

Albert stood up with Gracie but didn't let go of her. "Who's Cheryl Lee? Did Gracie know her? Why is she so upset by this?"

"Gracie did know her a little. This type of thing always bothers the other patients."

The orderly tugged at Albert's arms. He relented and put Gracie on the gurney. The orderly strapped her down and started slowly pushing it away while looking to the nurse for direction. Gracie started sobbing loudly then. Albert followed the orderly until Nurse Downer stopped him.

"Go home, Mr. Grant. We'll call you."

"But Gracie seems really thrown by this. She was doing better until she heard the news about this Cheryl Lee person. Nurse, what was their connection?"

Nurse Downer huffed and said, "Albert, please, you'll just have to trust us. We know the situation between this suicide victim and your wife. It could very well be that just the idea of suicide has thrown Gracie. She's a very sensitive woman, as you know. We will help her cope with this horrible development. Go home and wait to hear from us."

With that said, Nurse Downer turned and signaled the orderly to follow her with Gracie's gurney down the hall. Albert stood watching them go. Gracie's sobbing became fainter and fainter. People were all headed around and away from him now. The uproar was subsiding. *Good God*, Albert thought, *is a suicide like this just another day in this damned place?*

Albert sat in his truck in the hospital parking lot. Today's events swirled in his head. A mechanical Gracie on their visit. His shameful failure to perform well sexually—Gracie's fault for startling him so with her command request that was so unlike her. Suicide of someone whom Gracie obviously knew in some way and reacted so strongly to. He wondered if he would ever be able to take his wife home again. Would he dare to?

The bakery truck started with the first crank of the key and seemed to want to go north to Livermore to his sister's farm, or so Albert thought. He let it steer him. His Waynie would be napping at Mrs. Alley's house in Waterville at this time in the afternoon, so he would just go up and visit Steve and bum a Sunday meal off Ruth. Maybe some sympathy, too.

Chapter Forty-One

Gracie felt her best bet was to just float through all this. She didn't want to hear anyone. She didn't want to see or talk to anyone. Turned to the wall beside her cot, she resisted rolling over to look at the person trying to get Gracie to notice her. *Sounds like Nurse Downer. Maybe. Maybe not. Don't care, just floating. Need to go to the bathroom? Too late. Sorry. I'm just floating.*

Stronger shake. Harsher, older voice. *Leave me alone, Nurse Wight, you old battle-ax! Let me float! I don't want to play anymore!* Quiet now. Soon dark. Snoring.

"Gracie, Gracie don't do this to us! You can hear me, and I know it. Don't do this! Not to me, Gracie." No shaking. No attempt to roll her over, but there was someone there. Wouldn't leave when she ignored the request. *Damn you, Dr. Knowles, what are you doing here? I told you about the floating. Go away.*

Gracie thought all was quiet. Her left side was sore. She'd just switch sides while no one was around. When she did, she opened one eye. *Damn!*

"Hello, Gracie," said Dr. Knowles. "Done floating yet?"

"No," Gracie whispered. She squeezed her eyes shut.

"Well, my young lady, I have an appointment. Plus, I'm getting stiff in my joints from sitting here trying to wait you out. I want you to think about this. You can do this with your eyes closed if you wish. Think about all the work you and I have done and all the progress we've made. I know Cheryl Lee's suicide really bothered you, but is it worth throwing away all the improvement you've made? You need to stop that damned floating stuff and start responding soon, or we'll have to consider more shock treatments. I'm off. Think things over, Gracie."

Gracie felt the air move slightly as Dr. Knowles got up and left her bedside. She stayed on her right side for a long time. She felt wet again. It was uncomfortable. Her stomach growled. *Why can't I do this anymore? I used to be so good at it.* She sat up on her cot, pulled her knees up to her chest, and started crying.

"Are you back, Gracie?" that damned, sweet, familiar voice asked from behind her.

"Yes, I guess so," answered Gracie. "Why, Dena, why?"

"We don't know, do we?" Nurse Downer was now sitting on the empty cot next to her patient. "Cheryl Lee was always quite troubled, Gracie."

"Oh, we had an inkling, now didn't we?" Gracie glared sideways at the nurse. "Maybe someone should have taken her seriously?"

"Cheryl Lee liked to latch onto a new patient and tell her stories, Gracie. You were unfortunately her latest audience. Ask around among the other women here in your ward when some of them return. But right now, we need to change you and your bed, please. The smell is not pleasant."

Gracie was flabbergasted, but she decided to just play along with the nurse. She let her lead her into the shower room and help her take off her clothing. She noticed Nurse Downer peek at her underpants and then look up at her.

"Don't worry, Nurse, I haven't had a monthly since I've been here," she grumbled and turned to go under the shower head. She stood under the water for a long time. She rinsed away everything over and over again. When she did finally turn off the water, she noticed the nurse had left her a towel and a set of hospital clothes. Despair enveloped her once she had slipped into the hospital garb. She stumbled her way back to her cot in the ward. It was freshly made. A tray of soup and crackers set on the foot of it. Gracie picked up the tray carefully. Her stomach churned. Then she turned and flung the tray as hard as she could. It splattered against the opposite wall, decorating the two nearest cots. She didn't hear the gasps behind her since she was howling so fiercely. She did feel the arms that grabbed her roughly and held her while she felt a jab in her right thigh. She also heard the "Get her in isolation!" before blackness fell upon her.

Chapter Forty-Two

Giggles filled the farm air along with the constant smell of the manure pile mounded twenty feet from Ruth's back porch. Albert's nieces Linda and Minnie were walking fourteen-month-old Stevie around the bumpy driveway. He'd do pretty well while they allowed him to hold onto their hands. Once they let go, it was a matter of three or four steps before he landed on his diapered bottom. Usually Minnie, not many months older than her male cousin, would fall too. Linda, still standing at the ripe old age of four, would look around triumphantly. Then all three would squeal with laughter and start the process over again.

"You let me know when you're ready to talk, dear brother. I'll be sitting here beside you, like always." Ruth looked up and smiled at the children's shenanigans. "Those silly little ones. The girls will miss Stevie when he goes. They have such a time with him."

Albert sat with his elbows on his knees, his head down, and his hands flipping small rocks onto the patch of ground in front of the porch steps. Slightly more than a year older than Albert, Ruth had literally almost always been by his side until her wedding day. He'd missed her when she moved out of the Grant farmstead in Benton and up here to Livermore with her new husband's family. "I don't know what I'd do without you, Sis."

"Well, let's hope you never have to find out." They sat and watched their offspring and also looked over the dirt driveway to the orchard where Ruth's husband was driving an old tractor up and down lanes between trees.

"I should go help out Ernest," Albert announced. He started to get up. Ruth grabbed his arm and pulled him back down.

"No, he's fine. He likes riding around on that antique vehicle. Reminds him of his dad. Besides, don't take two men to pull down a few remaining apples. You sit with me and the little ones. You arrived at the farm this afternoon looking like the world had run over you."

"It did, Sis. I don't know if I'll ever get Gracie out of that hospital. She fell completely apart when she heard the news about a patient committing suicide. Didn't even get a chance to say goodbye to her. Linda and Minnie may never have to face saying goodbye to their cousin."

"If I was you, Al, I'd call the hospital and ask for a meeting with her doctor. See if you can make some sort of plan or have some notion of when he thinks she might be able to at least get out for a short while and visit her babies. I think that would make a world of difference to her. I really do."

"Maybe, Ruth, maybe. As delicate as she is, I'd be scared to take her away from there for too long. God, this is horrible!"

"Albert Russell Grant, what do you mean you're scared? You handled her before. You can again. Bring her up here to the farm if you'd like to. At least for a little while. I'll help you with her. I think we could do it together."

"I don't know. Lot to ask of Ernest. Let me think about it. Can I stay for supper?"

"Sunday night special, my dear: Shit on a shingle."

"Sounds good to me. Chipped beef on crackers is better then what I would pick up on the way back to Waterville."

Chapter Forty-Three

There she is again, mused Gracie as she listened to Nurse Downer chatter beside her cot in the isolation room. *Why doesn't she leave me alone?*

"I'm going to visit you every chance I get until you start talking to me, Gracie Grant!" Nurse Downer spoke close to Gracie's ear. "Don't you even think I'm going to throw away all the progress we made in the past couple months over what Cheryl Lee did. No, sirree! The hospital people are investigating that whole thing. They'll do something about it, Gracie, but you can't. Do you think Cheryl Lee would have wanted you to do whatever it is you're doing right now? Would she? I'm just sitting here until I have to go help Nurse Wight with meds. So there!"

"For the love of all that's holy, Dena!" Gracie opened her eyes and looked at the nurse's face that hovered within inches of her own. "What investigation are you talking about?"

"Welcome back," Nurse Downer smiled.

"Asshole with your welcome back," answered Gracie. "Don't want to be back."

"Well, you are now, aren't you?"

"Yes, for Christ's sake. I'm back. What investigation are you going on about?"

"Word has it through the grapevine that Dr. Knowles is furious with Dr. Getchell for not picking up on Cheryl Lee's suicidal tendencies. Old Nurse Wight said they had quite a fight."

Gracie stared at the nurse now. She didn't know whether to believe her or not. Nurse Downer stared right back at her and then asked, "Can I bring you back to the ward, Gracie? Are you ready to join us again?"

"What the hell?" Gracie sighed. "I suppose I'll have to. What else am I going to do?"

Patients were settling from supper in the ward as Nurse Downer led Gracie to her cot. Several looked up at Gracie. *Doe eyes. They have doe eyes, these poor people.* The nurse left Gracie sitting on her cot and ran off to help her superior with handing out medications. A patient who hadn't spoken since Gracie arrived in September quietly tiptoed over and sat next to her. She tentatively reached for one of Gracie's hands. She said nothing. Gracie patted her hand. The other patient smiled and nodded. "Yes, I'm back," Gracie told her.

Chapter Forty-Four

Route 4 was lined with bare trees this cold November morning as Albert wound his bakery truck down it after staying overnight at his sister's farm. He decided Ruth was right about asking more questions of the doctor at Augusta State Hospital. Gracie was his wife. He had a right to be involved in her treatment more than he had been so far. But he had to win a bit of Gracie's affection back in some way.

"So, the next time they let me visit Gracie, I'm going to have Ira John holding Waynie in the parking lot. You can see it from the window in the visitor's room. I'll take Gracie to the window to look at them. You know how she loves that little brother of hers, Alley," Albert said through a mouthful of apple pie. He had escaped Ruth's farm in the wee hours of the morning without breakfast.

"I don't know, Al," replied Mrs. Alley as she washed dishes at the sink. "Do you think she's ready for something like that?"

"Lord only knows, but she'll never be completely better if she stays in there. Another patient might do something crazy, and she would fall apart again. You know how sensitive she is."

"Maybe you're right," muttered Mrs. Alley at the plate she was rinsing off. "We can't let her stay there too long. We don't want her to lose hope and start acting like some of the other patients she's mixed in with, I guess."

"Ruth says I can take her up to the farm for a short while if I can get her out. I just don't know how long Ernest will let us stay."

"No, Al, you bring her back here. I can help handle her. She's been here before. A familiar place. If you and I can't handle her here, we'll know she shouldn't be out of the hospital."

"Listen, Alley, if I do get her out of that place, it will take hell freezing over for me to take her back." Albert stood with his hands on his hips now. His shoulders were thrown back.

"Never say never about anything. You don't know what life will throw at you." Mrs. Alley threw her dish towel over one shoulder. "Want another piece of breakfast pie, kid?"

Albert's shoulders drooped. "God, you're probably right. And yeah, I'll take another piece before you put it away, please. And Alley?"

"What now?"

"Thanks."

"Gobble that pie down and get to the bakery. The last thing you need to do is lose your job if you want to get Gracie back home. And don't sneak in to peek at Waynie. You might wake up some of the other critters, and I'll lose my few last moments of peace and quiet here."

Albert negotiated the stairs carefully, so he wouldn't wake up the houseful of children. He slipped into his Harris Bakery uniform. He felt better having a plan of action. He'd call Dr. Knowles later today. Mrs. Alley was reading the morning newspaper when he went back through the kitchen. He stopped and kissed the top of her head.

"Cut that out and get to work!" snapped Mrs. Alley. She turned her head to hide the grin on her face.

Chapter Forty-Five

"Miss Downer tells me you've been rather blue these past few days, Gracie."

Dr. Knowles waited. He received no reply. "I'm glad you at least came here for your appointment."

Gracie looked up at the doctor without saying a word. She got up and walked over to look out of his office window with no security screen. Dr. Knowles shuffled papers while keeping a sideways eye on his patient. She turned back and studied the doctor. "May I ask you a question about something that is supposedly none of my business?"

"If it will allow us to get back to our work afterwards, ask away, Gracie."

"Have you really done an investigation of Cheryl Lee's suicide, or is Nurse Downer just telling me that?"

"You're right about this not being your business. Let me just say this, Gracie. Nurse Downer isn't telling you stories just to appease you. People are being questioned. I can't tell you who they are, but please understand that we're upset about what happened. I'm sorry, Gracie. I really am." Dr. Knowles looked down at his hands. Gracie returned to her chair.

"Okay."

"Can we talk about your visit with your husband?"

"We're a pair, the two of us. Grace and Disgrace."

Dr. Knowles wrinkled his forehead and looked at Gracie. "I feel a story coming on."

"No big story, Doc. Just what my Grandpa John used to call Al and me. Nice, huh? And he was one person I thought really loved me. Old fool."

"Our records say that your grandfather suffers from hardening of the arteries and displays behavior that is less than rational. Did he have a good reason for calling you two such a mean name?"

"He started calling us that before we were married and before his funny spells. One day after Al had visited the farm and charmed my little cousins Shirl and Pat by shadow boxing, Grandpa had been rude to him, so I questioned the old man about his feelings for Al. I told him Al was from a God-fearing family that went to the same church he did. He said to me, 'Not all people inside a church are good people, Gracie. You'll learn that. Maybe the hard way hanging around with that Grant boy and getting involved with his family.'"

"Did you get him to explain what he meant?"

"Well, he kept saying things like, I didn't have any more brains than his stupid daughter Myrabelle. Told me my mother married a no-good man, and I probably would, too. I said that Al didn't drink like my father Kent. I asked him what he had against the Grants. He said Al's father was a business shyster from way back. Then he wouldn't say any more. Uncle Polly came in as he was talking to me and took issue with him saying something like that to me. Grandpa hollered at him too, and left the room. Try as he did, Al never could win his favor."

"But he tried to, did he?" Dr. Knowles asked.

"Yeah, he did. Seemed to bother him. He knew I was fond of my grandfather and all."

"Gracie, maybe your grandfather was starting not to think clearly at that point and not many people had noticed."

"Maybe."

"Maybe he was just fearful for you and worried about you getting into a bad situation like your mother had."

"Maybe, Doc. I don't know." Gracie looked down at her hands for a minute and then back up at Dr. Knowles.

"Gracie, have you noticed that when you speak to me these days you look at me instead of whispering while glancing at the floor like you used to do?" Dr. Knowles smiled.

"Did I really act crazy when I first arrived, Doc?"

"You don't remember what you were like when you first came to the hospital over two months ago?" Dr. Knowles put his arms on his desk and leaned toward his patient.

"No, Doc, I don't. Dena tells me about it, and it doesn't seem possible to me." Gracie leaned toward the doctor now.

"Dena?"

"You know, Nurse Downer. She's been good to me. She's persistent, that's for sure." Now Gracie smiled.

"Nurse Dena Downer is a bright, competent nurse whom this hospital is very lucky to have," replied Dr. Knowles. "She is very interested in your progress."

"I don't know why, Doc. Why would she care so much about the likes of me?"

"She sees potential in you, Gracie. You're young, very bright, and you have two young boys out there waiting for you to come home to them. And a husband who cares for you. She wants that, too."

Gracie stared back at Dr. Knowles. She turned sideways in her chair and looked out the window again.

"Gracie, want to tell me what you're thinking?"

"I need to sort it out in my own head first, Doc, but I do have a question."

"Ask it, by all means, Gracie."

"When you visited me last time in the ward, you mentioned shock therapy again. Do you think I need more treatments? I don't. I'm pretty rational now, I think. Lord, I can't even float anymore the way I used to be able to do."

Dr. Knowles looked down at his desk before looking back up at Gracie. "I was desperate and decided all I could do was try to scare you back, Gracie. I don't think you need more shock treatments. Saying that to you was wrong of me. I'm sorry."

Gracie sat up straight and looked carefully at the doctor. "Not many people have ever said something like that to me, Doc. Never said sorry for anything."

"Someone should have by now, Gracie. You've suffered through a lot of hard times."

"Al did, I guess," Gracie had her legs crossed and swung her top leg a bit. "I'm afraid I have to admit that my Al did say that a few times."

"Can we talk about your Albert at some point?"

"Yeah, but not today. I'm really tired, Doc." Gracie uncrossed her legs and slouched.

"Okay, another day soon. I'm glad you're back with us, Gracie."

"What the hell else am I going to do, Doc?"

"You know what else, and you've tried it, too," Dr. Knowles said a bit loudly.

Gracie wrapped her arms around herself and looked at the floor. Then she glanced up at the doctor. "I know, Doc. I'm sorry about that."

"Off with you now, Gracie. Get something to eat. You're still skin and bones," Dr. Knowles said as Gracie had already gotten up from her chair and headed to the door.

Chapter Forty-Six

Aunt Edie looked concerned as Albert talked at her supper table in her Windsor home about his plan to have Ira John go to Augusta with him and Waynie on Sunday. Uncie watched his wife Edie. Ira John was all grins as they passed bowls of mashed potatoes and squash around.

"I don't know what I think about this idea, Al. Ira John is only a kid," said Aunt Edie. "I don't think it's a good thing for him to be exposed to that place."

"First of all, I told everyone I wanted to be called Johnny now. And secondly, I'm not a baby, Aunt Edie. I want to go see my sister, for heaven's sake," said Johnny. He started wolfing down potatoes.

"I need some help here getting your niece out of 'that place,' Edie," Albert said. "Johnny is like a tonic to Gracie. He won't be going into the hospital. He's not allowed and certainly not Waynie, either. They would simply wave at Gracie from the parking lot like I explained. I'm worried she's been away from her boys so long, they seem unreal to her," Albert joined Johnny in eating some potatoes. "Tastes good, Edie. Please tell me you'll think about it."

"Nothing for her to think about, Al. I'm doing it whether or not Aunt Edie wants me to. My sister would do anything for me." Johnny looked over at his aunt with a steady glare. "Least I can do is help Al with this idea."

"Now, now, young man! You don't talk to your aunt that way," said Uncie. "You're still living under our roof, you know."

"Don't want to cause a fight here," said Albert. "But I'm desperate. I need help. I really think Gracie would respond positively to seeing Johnny and Waynie even if it's just from a window."

Awkward silence filled the small dining area of the farmhouse now. Everyone was chewing quietly. Edie put her fork down with food still on her plate. She excused herself and went to the kitchen. The three men finished the meals on their plates while glancing back and forth at one another.

Uncie jumped up and announced that Johnny needed to help him in the barn. Albert grabbed plates and headed to the kitchen. He found Edie there crying while standing at the sink. "Al, some of this is my fault. I should have argued more with Uncie about taking Gracie, when we grabbed Ira John years ago. I thought I could eventually convince him to let me take her once we had her little brother settled. I know things weren't perfect with her mother's relatives, but I never realized how much we hurt her by leaving her to them. God will make me pay for this, I know it."

"It was your brother Kent who abused her, Edie. You didn't have anything to do with that, now did you?" Albert started piling the dishes by the sink.

"I knew Kent was no good. We all knew and did nothing about it. Uncie claimed it was Kent's house, and we had no business sticking our noses in it. I should have spoken up. Especially after the older three were taken by the town fathers and the minister. Then along came sweet, little Ira John. Oh, God, when I think now of the shack right down the road those children spent precious years in. Old, drunken Jackknife Fred helped them more than Uncie and I did until Myrabelle finally fell so sick that Bernice and Georgette took her to the sanitarium. I didn't do what I should have."

Albert towered over tiny Edie Reed now as he stood with his eyes closed beside her at the sink. Then he opened them and spoke up. "Edie, past is past. No use fussing over it. You have a chance now to help me get our Gracie out of that hospital. I want to come here early Sunday afternoon with Waynie and pick up Johnny. I'll take them both to the hospital with me. Will you let me do that, please?"

Edie was wringing her hands now. "Yes, Al, I will. Please tell me you'll be careful with what details about Gracie's illness you share with Ira John. Remember he's just a fifteen-year-old boy."

Albert hugged Edie and said, "I've been cautious about what I'm telling him, but he's smart. He already knows more than you think. I'll be very careful with both boys."

"What about little Stevie?"

"He's at my sister Ruth's farm now. I wanted to give Mrs. Alley a break. I'll start with Johnny and Waynie first. Maybe the next week she'll want to see the baby, too."

They looked up to see Uncie and Ira John peering at them from the back door. Johnny was grinning from ear to ear.

Chapter Forty-Seven

Gracie looked around the ward each night after supper for Gus, the attendant who had threatened Cheryl Lee and scared her as well. He didn't appear for his usual shift for almost a week. The next morning, Gracie caught Nurse Downer at the medicine cart.

"Dena, what happened to Gus who works the evening shift? Haven't seen him for days." Gracie watched the nurse dole out pills.

"Gracie, don't jump to conclusions, but everyone says Dr. Knowles had him fired. Nurse Wight said Gus left in a big huff. I'm not sure what happened and don't ask me anything about Dr. Getchell. Nurse Wight just looks funny when I ask her about the fight between him and Knowles. She was there when Knowles questioned him about inappropriate behavior." Nurse Downer glanced around after she stopped speaking.

"Can Dr. Knowles get another doctor fired around here?"

"Gracie, Dr. Getchell is just a resident here. He's not a full doctor. I believe Dr. Knowles can do whatever he feels is necessary to do about him. Getchell is not looking too happy lately. I wouldn't mind if he left us."

"Oh, I thought you'd rather cottoned to Getchell as he was so handsome, Dena?"

Miss Downer grabbed Gracie and spoke close to her face. "Gracie, I'm just another woman in this place, like you. Getchell is a flirt. I couldn't afford to risk my job by being mean to him or rebuffing his advances, you know. I have to play the game, too."

"Okay, Dena, I see that," said Gracie, pulling back from Nurse Downer. "I think you are a bit higher up on the food chain than I am, but I do understand what you're saying. You've never stepped out with him?"

"Of course not! We nurses all know Getchell wants just one thing. We pretend to flirt back and then keep our distance. I didn't realize that when he was first here. Thought maybe marrying a doctor would be nice, but I learned quickly marriage is not in that one's vocabulary."

Gracie watched the nurse now. "What do you suppose he did with Cheryl Lee during their therapy sessions?"

"Don't go down that road, Gracie! You don't know, and neither do I. I'm hoping he pays for it by losing his position here, but I have no influence over that decision. You don't either, so don't go questioning Dr. Knowles during your sessions with him. You know how men are? They'll do what they want to do about things, and we have very little say in that."

"Oh, don't I ever know that, Dena!" Gracie put her hand on Dena's shoulder. "Don't I ever."

Miss Downer reached out and hugged Gracie then pushed her slightly away and asked her, "Gracie, would you like your job in the library back? It would get you out of the laundry room again. Mrs. Philbrook spoke to me this morning about not knowing that you were only concerned about Cheryl Lee and not really in cahoots with her. What do you think? Say yes, please! It would make Dr. Knowles think you are feeling better."

Gracie managed a quiet yes, and Nurse Downer hugged her again. "Gracie, your session is in a few minutes. Do you want to get out of this place by Christmas?"

"I guess so, why?"

"Answer every question the doctor asks you and do ask about your little boys."

"Waynie and Stevie?"

"Yes, those two. Now go on."

Gracie's head ached as she walked fast through the tunnel that connected the wards with the offices. *What if I could have done more to help poor Cheryl Lee? Why do I feel so horrible about getting my library job back? Is it at Cheryl Lee's expense? Stop it and think about yourself for once, Grace Murray Grant!*

Gracie knocked on Dr. Knowles' door. "Who's there?" she heard from the other side of the door. *Play the game. Even Dena has to play the game.*

"It's me, Dr. Knowles."

"Me who?" came back in a joking tone.

Okay, Gracie, you can do this, too. "Your very favorite patient, Doc, that's who."

"Well, then come on in."

Gracie ran her fingers through her hair and straightened her dress. She walked into the office with her head held high. She took her usual look out of the doctor's picturesque window before taking her seat on the chair in front of the doctor's desk.

"Hi, Gracie. I believe we had a plan for today's session, didn't we?"

"We did, Doc. Where do you want me to start?"

"Gracie, can you tell me why you feel unwanted?"

"That's easy; no one ever wanted me. Two town fathers and the local minister came into our house in 1924 when I was an infant. They took my two older sisters and brother and left me there. Cora talks about how she remembers what happened. Tells me it was soon after I was born. Our mother thought our old man had come home drunk after hearing noises in the yard. She had Cora take Flippie and Ken and scoot under my parent's bed. Put me in a box with a blanket and shoved it under there, too. Cora said our mother told her to keep everyone quiet and to stick her finger in my mouth if I started crying. But it wasn't the old man at all. It was the men who took them all away except for me. Cora insists that she heard them say something about going back for me when I was weaned. Laughed about how she didn't know what that meant at the time. I don't know if I believe her or not. Doesn't matter. They never went back for me. That's that."

"How old were your siblings at the time, Gracie?"

"Cora was five, and Flippie and Ken were three and two. They insist they remember that, too. I believe Cora, but how could two toddlers remember something like that when they were so young, Doc?"

"Memories of traumatic things like that are funny, Gracie. They may just remember being scared. Not as likely that they would remember details like Cora did. Why do you think they never came back and grabbed you?"

"Never asked, Doc. I was busy trying to survive with my poor mother. She was crippled on one side, you know. Then, when I was eight, along came Ira John. Damned old bastard Kent was never around when we were cold or hungry, but he came around every once in a while for that, now didn't he!"

"You've said you had to help a great deal with raising your little brother," remarked the doctor.

"God, yes, I guess I did. Our mother couldn't run after him. She had a hard time just walking. Spent four years chasing that little bugger around 'til Aunt Edie and Uncie took him when my mother became too ill to stay home."

"How do you feel about them not taking you, too?"

"Mad as hell! How do you think I feel? I was always the one left behind. Poor little Gracie. That's me." She looked up suddenly at the doctor. "I'm sorry for yelling, Doc."

"That's okay, Gracie. It's good to see you show some serious emotion here. It's time to air out your feelings."

Not all of them, Doc, thought Gracie. *But some of them.* She gazed out the window.

"Gracie, have you ever talked about any of this with Albert?"

"Some, I guess. Some of this. Why?"

"Gracie, he seems to care about you. He's called to make an appointment with me this week."

"Why?" Gracie's frown was deep and troubled.

"I think he worries about you. Nurse who took the call says he wants to talk about your progress. What do you think about that?"

"Probably wants a hot meal, his house cleaned, and his boys taken care of again, is what I think, Doc."

Dr. Knowles moved around in his seat. He crossed his legs. He frowned back at Gracie. "He has that right now at Mrs. Alley's place. Do you think he might be actually concerned about you?"

Gracie looked at her hands and didn't answer.

"Do you love him, Gracie?"

"Does it matter, Doc? We're married with two kids. I'm his, I guess. His old man pounded responsibility into his poor head from day one. He can probably still hear him talking from the grave, for Christ's sake. He'd worry about me because that is what is expected of him. I can hear Mother Grant right now; I know what she'd be saying to him. 'You took marriage vows in front of God himself, Albert. Now you keep those promises.'" Gracie paused and laughed. "Oh, how she used to go after him when we lived at the farm with them."

"Sounds like you have a bit of sympathy for Albert."

"I suppose so. Poor, pretty-faced little shit. He could have gone on to school. He was smart, too, you know. His old man wouldn't hear of it. No sir! Albert was to stay on the farm and help with the family business. God!"

"What happened to his father?"

"Dropped dead in the car coming home from church services. Heart stuff, they said. Was sixty. Al's mother was younger than him. And then we lost the farm. I was glad. Mother Grant went to live with Al's sister Mollie to take care of her daughter."

"Al's had it rather hard, too, hasn't he?" asked the doctor.

"I guess so. Do you really think he cares about me, Doc?"

"I think maybe he does. I'm worried about what you think about him, though. You know it will take some time to sort out your feelings about him and your boys."

"I want to get out of here and take care of my boys, Doc. I do!" Gracie sat up on the edge of her chair now and looked straight at the doctor. "I miss my Waynie and Stevie. Do you believe me?"

"I do, Gracie. I believe you. Now what I want you to do is think about your feelings about Albert. If you can, think about this situation a little bit from his point of view. Can you do that?

"Maybe," Gracie said and then sighed.

"Tired?"

"Yes, very tired."

"I am very proud of you for what you opened up about today, Gracie. You go take it easy. Think things over. Okay?" Gracie nodded, got up, and scurried out of the office. She paused on the other side of the door. Her head ached even more than when she had gone in.

Chapter Forty-Eight

Gracie loved being among the stacks at the tiny hospital library again. She loved to read and considered herself a pretty good writer. Lately, she could actually focus on reading. It was a sheer delight to have that ability return to her. Now, if she could only figure out how she could go back to Albert as if nothing had happened and carry on with the family. She was lost in thought when Mrs. Philbrook whisper-hollered at her from the front desk.

"Gracie, your visitor has arrived. You're needed in the visitors' lounge. Better hurry. Always nice to have visitors, my dear."

Good God, thought Gracie, *I forgot it was Sunday!* She muttered to herself about not being able to function without her buddy Dena as she hustled to the bathroom. She repinned her hair and pinched some color into her cheeks. *Oh, for a little dab of Dena's lipstick!* She scurried off to the lounge.

Gracie couldn't find Albert when she first entered the room filled with patients and visitors. Then she spied him. He was at the big window on the side of the room. She stood looking at the back of this man. Except for those broad shoulders, Albert was a small man. Rugged for his size, he always bragged to people. Gracie searched her heart for feelings. *Where are they,* thought Gracie? *Why do I still feel nothing?*

Albert turned around and smiled his boyish grin. "Gracie, come! I have a surprise for you. Come look out the window with me."

Gracie hesitated. She had no idea what to expect to see out the window. She walked over slowly. Albert stood close to her now, but he didn't touch her. He just kept grinning and asking her to look out the window and down at the ground. She looked. She froze and grabbed her face with both hands. She trembled ever so slightly. Albert looked startled and concerned now.

"They wanted to say hello and see you, but they're too young to come visit you in here. This was the next best thing, I thought. Are you okay?" Albert now touched Gracie's back gently.

"Yes, Al, yes, I'm okay. Look at them! Waynie looks so grownup now. And my Ira John. My sweet Ira John. I didn't know he knew I was in here, Al."

"He's been really worried about you, Gracie. Why wouldn't he be? You're like his mother, you know."

"Well, there's Aunt Edie now, isn't there."

"You tell that little fart that, Gracie. He loves you."

"Look at my Waynie. Is he out of diapers now?"

"Sure is! Very proud of himself, too. Talking a blue streak."

"How about the baby, Al? Where's he?"

"Ruth is taking care of Stevie just temporarily, Gracie. I thought it best to give Alley a bit of a break, you know."

"Alley? Heavens, she lets you call her that, doesn't she? She'd snatch anyone else bald for not calling her Mrs. Alley. Just you, Albert." Now Gracie grinned, too. Albert put his arm around her shoulders, and Gracie allowed herself to snuggle against him the tiniest bit. Then she pulled back and faced him. "Albert, you didn't give Stevie to Ruth and Ernest, did you? I know they would love to have a boy!"

"Of course not, Gracie. I made it plain that it was only temporary. Linda and Minnie mind him mostly up there. You know how busy that farm keeps Ruth."

Gracie settled back against Albert now. "Okay, Al. You better not be lying to me."

She watched her two boys out the window as they waved up at her. She giggled as Ira John held Waynie on his shoulders and marched around in front of Al's bakery truck. Then she laughed out loud when Ira John put his nephew down, and Waynie marched around behind his uncle. They both clowned around a bit as if they were putting on a show for Gracie.

"Dr. Knowles said you had called and asked for an appointment to see him. Is that true, Al?"

"Well, yes, I wanted to know how soon you would be able to come home to us, Gracie. Is that okay?"

"Do you really want me back home?"

"Of course, I do, Gracie. Why wouldn't I want you home?"

Gracie stared into his face now. Albert turned and looked out the window. They stood for a few more minutes watching the young ones' antics. Then Albert spoke up. "Gracie, I have to get Ira John back to Windsor, so I need to get going. Promised Edie I wouldn't have him out for long."

"I'm sure my illness has her in a tizzy. Probably afraid I'll start taking after her brother and be a mess, too. Poor Aunt Edie."

"Oh, no, Gracie, I think she really does love you. She just doesn't like talking about these things, is all. Uncie doesn't know what to think. Edie feels badly that you've had it so hard."

Gracie glared back at Albert. He kissed her forehead and said goodbye. She watched him walk out of the room. Then she looked back at Ira John and Waynie. She moved closer to the window and pressed her hands and face against it. Feelings filled her heart now. She just didn't know how to sort them all out. She pushed back and waved as Albert got them in the truck. She watched the truck for as long as she could see it and stayed against the window for a few more minutes until she heard a friendly voice.

"Gracie, did I miss seeing them? Darn it all." Gracie turned to her friend Dena. She smiled and hugged her.

"I guess you enjoyed your visit, did you?"

"Yes, I did. I want to go home, Dena. I want to go home."

Chapter Forty-Nine

Albert felt foolish waiting in the doctor's office with his Harris Bakery uniform on, but he hadn't had a chance to change out of it before he was due at the hospital to see Dr. Knowles.

He was looking out the big window in the doctor's office when the doctor came in.

"Hi, Albert. Sorry I'm late. Afraid I'm always late. Story of my life around here in this big place." He held out his hand for Albert to shake. "Please sit down if you can tear yourself away from that view. Best part of this office. Your wife loves looking out of that window."

Albert sat down. "Does she sit in this chair, too?"

"Yes, she does, as a matter of fact. Now, you and I need to talk business here. Your wife is a lot better, Al. What are your thoughts about her having a trial visit at home?"

Albert tried not to look too surprised. "Do you really think she is doing better, Doc? She really fell apart with the news of that woman committing suicide, but she did seem okay this past Sunday, I guess. You think she is ready for a trial visit home?"

"I do. She was very upset by her fellow patient's suicide, but in a way that was almost a sign of her health being better, if you can understand what I mean. She reacted strongly like a person who was well enough to have the proper empathy about the occurrence. It didn't take her long to be able to settle down and get back to her therapy here."

"I see. It just startled me to have her fall apart like that. She's always been sensitive, but her going back into that state where she refuses to talk really scared me."

"She didn't stay there for very long this time, Al. That's a good sign, believe me."

Albert shook his head now and cleared his throat. "When do you think she'll be ready for this trial you're talking about?"

"We'll have to have a board review here at the hospital. I need to convince them she is ready. She'll have to be able to sit in front of them and speak well. I think we can do this. I need to have a couple things in place from you, Al."

"Do I need to come here for the meeting?"

"No, but you do need to have a place ready for her to go to where she'll have 'round the clock supervision. It won't be wise for her to be alone for quite a while. Or be alone with your boys. She'll need to ease back into caring for them and doing household chores. Can you manage that?"

"Of course, Doc. Already have Alley, I mean Mrs. Alley, ready to take her back in and help her. We've talked about it just recently."

"You're lucky to have that lady. She sounds like a character on the phone, but a good-hearted one." Dr. Knowles smiled now.

"Don't know what I'd do without her. I really don't."

"I'll need a note from Mrs. Alley stating clearly that she is willing to have Gracie and help her for this trial period. Can you get her to send me one, please?"

"I sure can, Dr. Knowles. Right away. Anything else I need to do?"

"Actually, there is. Have you thought about letting Gracie get her license sometime in the future when she's better? She's a bright woman, and she feels trapped at home all day with two young boys. I really think being able to get out of the house on her own would be good for her mental health."

"Okay, Doc. I'll think about it. Anything to keep her better. Anything else?"

"Not for now. Get me that letter, and I'll keep you posted on her release. Any questions about Gracie from your end?"

"No, sir. Thank you." Albert jumped up and stuck his hand out to shake before saying goodbye and exiting the room.

Dr. Knowles sat and mused about the situation until Nurse Wight banged on his office door with a request for his help.

Within a few days, a letter was sitting on Dr. Knowles' desk. It was postmarked from Waterville. The doctor couldn't help but smile as he read the tiny, handwritten scrawl over two pages of stationery. It read:

> Dear Dr. Knowles,
>
> I am writing you in regard to Grace Grant. I am very much interested in her care as she seems like an own daughter of mine as she lived with me for 4 years before she was married and I also took care of her 4 weeks before she was admitted to the Hospital. I have her 2 boys with me and I expect to have her when she is discharged from the Hospital as I understand from her Husband that she is to be discharged from the Hospital in about 2 weeks. I would like very much for you to tell me all the facts about the case and also in what things I have to get prepared to be on the lookout for. If there is anything to be on the lookout for I will be prepared to expect most anything. I think of it in this way as I have the 2 children with me to take care of along with her when she is discharged. Please advise as to matters of importance. Will she ever have any more of the attacks again? I want the plain facts and no beating around the bush. Will she be discharged in about 2 weeks. Please advise.

> Yours,
> Mrs. Charles F. Alley
> Boutelle Ave
> Waterville
>
> P.S. She improving any at present and when will she be discharged.

"Mrs. Charles F. Alley, you are just what the doctor ordered," said Dr. Knowles to himself.

Chapter Fifty

Gracie glanced back and forth at the panel of four men and one woman. She was positioned in a straight-backed, wooden chair in front of them like some court defendant. At least she knew, didn't like but knew, the woman at the table. Nurse Wight glared out at her like a school principal. Dr. Knowles had told Gracie he would be with her. An empty chair was beside her. She really wanted to bring Dena with her after the sweet lady helped her get ready, but Dena told her she didn't need her. "You're ready for this!" she'd chided Gracie as she pushed her toward the meeting room door a few minutes earlier.

"I'm sorry, I'm sorry, dear gentlemen. And dear lady." Dr. Knowles swooped in the door behind Gracie and plunked himself in the chair next to her. "Gracie, have you met everyone?"

Before Gracie could answer, Dr. Knowles started giving elaborate introductions. He ended with her. "This is Grace Grant, a patient whom I feel is more than ready for a trial visit home." He smiled broadly at the entire panel. "Shall we start?"

"Mrs. Grant, how are you feeling?" asked a stout, gray-haired man in the middle of the panel.

Gracie peeked at Dr. Knowles. He nodded. Gracie replied, "I feel fine, sir. I want to go home to my husband and two boys. I'm ready to take care of my house and family now."

"How are you getting on here in the hospital lately? I see you were involved in a few skirmishes when you were first here," said the same man who appeared to be acting as a spokesman for the group.

"I'm fine. I love my job in the library, and I get along with everyone."

"I'd say you love your library," chimed in Nurse Wight. "Gentlemen, Grace has books and magazines cluttering her space so much, it is hard to change her bed."

"Nurse Wight, how wonderful it is that the patient is well enough to enjoy books and magazines. Perhaps she should be responsible for her bed being changed, so the reading material won't be a problem," replied the stout spokesman.

Dr. Knowles suppressed a laugh and smiled at Gracie. "The patient's mental capacity seems to have returned. It is indeed something to be happy about."

"Dr. Knowles, how many electroshock treatments were needed to help the patient regain herself?" asked another gentleman on the panel.

"We administered twenty-one treatments in three series of seven, sir. Gracie responded positively to the very first treatment and started talking again, but as to be expected, she suffered a few setbacks."

Gracie looked sideways at the doctor now. She started to wring her hands. Dr. Knowles reached for her left arm and asked her, "Gracie, do you feel markedly better now than you did when you first arrived at the hospital?"

"I think so, Doc," replied Gracie. "I don't really remember much about when I was first here."

"Of course, Gracie. You see, gentlemen and Nurse Wight, this loss of memory is an expected result of the shock therapy. Gracie was in a deep catatonic state upon being committed in September. We felt the aggressive treatment was warranted. Her memory will probably come back slowly as she continues to regain her health. I can vouch for the fact that Gracie has come a long way in her recovery with us. I feel a trial visit home will act as a wonderful tonic for her at this point."

"Are we assured she will continue to be under supervision, Doctor?" asked one of the men who hadn't to that point spoken up.

"We are. I have written assurance of that from a close family friend. Gracie and her family will be staying with this person for as long as she needs help."

Dr. Knowles continued to hold Gracie's left forearm gently, and Gracie calmed down and smiled at the panel.

The man who had started the conversation now looked at the people who sat on both sides of him. "I see no reason not to have full confidence in Dr. Knowles' opinion on this matter. Mrs. Albert Grant, you will be granted a trial visit home as soon as it can be arranged. We are finished here. Thank you, everyone." He rose from his chair with his salutation, and the others followed him.

Nurse Wight stopped in front of Dr. Knowles and Gracie as they stood in front of their chairs. "Gracie, you have improved a great deal, but you need to take good care of yourself. Promise you'll try to eat well and get the rest you need to fully recover, you hear?"

"Yes, I promise. Thank you," said Gracie as she bowed her head.

"Don't thank me, child. Thank that dear woman who has promised to take care of you until you get your sea legs under you." With that, Nurse Wight huffed, turned, and scurried out of the room.

Now Dr. Knowles laughed out loud. "Oh, that Nurse Wight! She is a piece of work. But a caring one, Gracie. One has to say that for her." Gracie looked up at him.

"I guess so, Doc. She doesn't always seem it, but she did today." Gracie looked up at the door the nurse had hustled out now. "Who would of thought it?"

"Gracie, a week from Sunday is when your husband and Mrs. Alley can come pick you up. You go back to your messy space and start wrapping your head around that. I'll see you for one more very quick session before you go."

Gracie sat on her bed. Lost in thought, she didn't hear Dena sneak up behind her, circle around her bed, and plunk down beside her until she was literally jiggled by the bounce of her mattress. "Jesus, Dena! Scare me to death!"

"Enough of that!" said Dena. "You getting out, or what?"

"Yes, a week from Sunday, I guess."

"What good news, Gracie!" Dena reached out and hugged Gracie.

"You anxious to get rid of me?"

"I'll miss you, but not enough to try to keep you here."

"What will I do out there, Dena?"

"You'll do one day at a time, Gracie. That's all. Come, Mrs. Philbrook says she has a project for you in the library. Think she's just anxious to hear how your board meeting went. Let's go tell her."

Dena jumped up and started off. "Come on, Gracie. Time to go!"

Gracie got up and followed her friend.

Chapter Fifty-One

The days went by quickly until the official Sunday of Gracie's release arrived. Her last session with Dr. Knowles was quick and almost dismissive, Gracie thought. Dena had the day off, but she promised Gracie she would stop by the hospital after lunch to say goodbye. Gracie waited for her on her bed. Her meager belongings were in a paper bag beside her. She had written her address down on a piece of paper to give to Dena. She hoped she might keep in touch with her. An attendant called for her.

Albert and Mrs. Alley were sitting in the waiting room. They were sporting their Sunday best for the occasion. Albert rocked back and forth in his chair. "Alley, do you still think it was wise to get Stevie back from Ruth's farm? Gracie had some serious qualms about that baby."

"Calm down, kid. You told me several times she was worried about Ruth and her husband trying to keep him. Seeing him back in Waterville will be a good thing. Now stop that infernal rocking, for God's sake!"

Albert was still for a couple minutes, but started rocking again just as an older nurse came into the waiting room and asked for him. Having his name called startled him. "What do you need?" he asked.

"We need to get you to sign something, Mr. Grant. Please follow me." The nurse turned and walked toward the door without waiting to make sure Albert was following him.

"Go on now, Al. Take care of whatever they need. I'll be here when they bring Gracie in if you're not back," said Mrs. Alley, giving Albert a less-than-gentle shove on his back.

Albert read over the paper that had been left on the desk in Dr. Knowles' office. It outlined that this was a trial visit home for Gracie in his custody. The trial was for a six month period. Albert was to sign this letter of promise stating that he would bring Gracie back to the hospital if any of her symptoms of illness returned. He paused for a minute while he held the pen in his hand.

"Mr. Grant, your wife has arrived in the waiting room. Are you all set there?" asked Nurse Wight as he stood in the office doorway.

"What does this mean?" Albert searched the nurse's face.

"You're taking responsibility for your wife, young man. You need to bring her back if she has any future problems just as it says. Are you okay with that?"

"Yes." His hand moved over the paper, scrawling his name in a messy fashion. He turned and followed the nurse back to the waiting room. There was his Gracie in a bear hug of Mrs. Alley's making.

"Al, doesn't she look great!" remarked Mrs. Alley as Gracie stepped back from her to look at Albert.

"Yes, she certainly does, Alley," said Albert as he smiled at both of them.

"There you are, Gracie!" Dena's voice interrupted them. "I was afraid I had missed you." Dena gave Gracie a firm hug. Gracie almost dropped the paper with her address on it. She handed it to Dena once she had released her from the embrace.

"Thanks, Gracie. I'll write. Promise. Be good now!"

Dena ran out of the room. "That's what she told me the first day I met her," said Gracie to Mrs. Alley and her husband.

"You remember that, dear?" asked Mrs. Alley.

"I do. At least that, I do. Some things I can't."

"Might be for the best, sweetheart," chirped Mrs. Alley. "Let's get you home."

Mrs. Alley grabbed Gracie's paper bag of things and started toward the door. Albert hung back with Gracie. He held his arm out for her to take.

Gracie put her arm in Albert's, but she hesitated. "What did you have to sign in Dr. Knowles' office, Al?"

Albert looked at his young wife. She studied his face for a few seconds. "Oh, Gracie, it was something to be proud of now."

"What?" Gracie looked at him. She wrinkled her brow.

"Gracie, it was a letter of sanity."

With that, they followed Mrs. Alley out.

Afterword

The "letter of sanity" was something Gracie clung to in years to come. When she ran into prejudice stemming from her stay at the Augusta State Hospital, she would refer to it and tell people she had proof of her sanity. Did they have the same? My brothers and I always thought it existed. I was disappointed when I didn't find it in the hospital records I received in 2012. It was the ultimate example of the protective bubble my father put her in and kept her as best he could over the years of fights and marital separations until his death in 1978.

Gracie never returned to the hospital although her illness would haunt her from time to time. Fortunately, she never experienced a psychotic break as severe as she had in 1948. With Mrs. Alley's and others' help, she did get better. In 1952 against her family doctor's advice, she had a daughter she named in honor of her hospital friend Cheryl Lee—the same Cheryl Lee Grant Gillespie who has written this book. I was the baby who would save her marriage and brighten her life. It was a challenging assignment that I'm still trying to resolve. Gracie did get her driver's license and proceeded to drive as much as she could with what my father called her "lead foot." There were many times when she did seem happy. At other times, my father, brothers, and I all watched her struggle and felt helpless as to how to help her.

Gracie's health deteriorated rapidly after my father's death, both physically and mentally. Those six years were difficult for both of us. My brothers lived out of state, so I was her caretaker. Her death in 1984 was questionable. She technically had a stroke, fell on her face, and lost consciousness, but pills were found in her toilet with an empty pill bottle open in the sink. Many pills were unaccounted for, but the doctor suggested a toxicology was really unnecessary. We all knew Gracie was tired of this world. She left us three days after the stroke. She had picked fights with everyone, and the discomfort was palpable at her funeral.

Gracie, I know you loved me as best you could. I loved you, too.

Acknowledgements

This book bubbled into existence over the course of nineteen years! It took many different forms and sat idle for many months here and there and even took a few years' hiatus. During that long period of time, many people helped and encouraged me to keep going with it. I have been involved in many different, helpful writing groups, classes, and workshops at Maine Writers and Publishers Alliance and the Maine Women Writers Collection of University of New England. The one group that helped me finally bring this to fruition included Cynthia Graves, Sue Morin, and Pat Walsh. Finally, I would like to thank my family—dear daughters Darcie Gillespie Hohwald and Kelsey Grace Gillespie, and my beloved husband John Gillespie, without whose love and encouragement this would not have been possible.

www.ingramcontent.com/pod-product-compliance
Lightning Source LLC
Chambersburg PA
CBHW071344080526
44587CB00017B/2963